REAL ESTATE MILLIONAIRE
Secrets

The Real Beginner's Guide to Real Estate

Noelle Randall, MPS, MBA

WALTON
PUBLISHING HOUSE

Walton Publishing House
Houston, Texas
www.waltonpublishinghouse.com
Printed in the United States of America

The advice found within may not be suitable for every individual. This work is purchased with the understanding that neither the author nor the publisher are held responsible for any results. Neither author nor publisher assumes responsibility for errors, omissions, or contrary interpretations of the subject matter herein. Any perceived disparagement of an individual or organization is a misinterpretation.

Brand and product names mentioned are trademarks that belong solely to their respective owners. Library of Congress Cataloging-in-Publication Data under ISBN: 978-1-953993-11-3

CONTENTS

To my children,

You all are what motivated me to overcome my struggles and become the person I am today. I know you will all be successful and will be able to do anything you set your minds to in life. I am so proud to call myself your mother.

INTRODUCTION

Greetings Future Millionaire!

First, I want to sincerely thank you for taking the time to pick up a copy of my book. I have been working on something special just for you, and I can't wait to hear your testimonial on how these principles and tools in this book helped set you on the path to making your first million dollars in real estate. I am excited about your future because I am certain that after you finish reading *Real Estate Millionaire Secrets*, your life is going to change. Yes, I know that is a bold statement, and I am sure this may not be the first time you've heard someone say something like this. But I am positive that this time the words you read on these pages will transform your life. I have poured my heart into this content, and I have applied an easy to follow yet applicable formula to help you learn the basics of creating your real estate investment business.

It's no secret that I love real estate. But more importantly than just real estate itself, I love the freedom that it has allowed me to experience in the course of a few short years. It has offered me the ability to position my family for generational wealth. I also love that real estate has been used as a vehicle to help me shift the trajectory of thousands of lives—the people who trust my brand and me. I couldn't imagine myself doing anything else. I am truly walking in my purpose.

So, should I go ahead and address the real estate skeptics early on that decided to pick up this book? I know some of you may be giving me the side-eye, and you purchased this book just so you can pick it apart and challenge the content. That's okay. I am glad you're here as well. If you stick around me long enough, you'll become a millionaire by association and proximity.

For those of you still reading, I am sure you have questions, so I'll go ahead and answer the most frequently asked one, "What makes what you're going to say any different than what I already know about real estate?" Well, that's a good question, and I am glad you asked. I believe that every good teacher or coach has a niche. My niche is helping real estate students identify the method of investing in real estate that best suits them and allows them to unlock massive results and profits in the process. My experience encompasses so many aspects of real estate, and I want to pass my knowledge on to you. I have been fortunate to find success while staying ahead of some of the biggest real estate market predictions. I have been humbled through the pitfalls, and I have celebrated big achievements. In other words, I am in the same "real estate" streets that you are (or will be) working in.

What I have experienced in my real estate journey is more than just textbook knowledge and including a few strategies that I copied from someone else. I have tested and learned where the gold mines are and how easy it really is to grow as a real estate investor when you take the time to become dedicated, when you take the business seriously, and when you learn all aspects of the business. I believe the best CEOs are those who have the knowledge to work every role in their organization. Like any business, there are many parts to real estate. In *Real Estate Millionaire Secrets* we'll be taking a deep dive into areas I think are the best to focus on for any new real estate investor. This business has caused me to grow in more ways than I can imagine, and I have become a better and wiser person in the process. I want you to experience this as well.

I don't want you to make the same mistakes I did. I want you to win!

I believe that if I can do it, then so can you. Did you know that I was able to build my real estate business while having a negative bank account? Yes, you read that correctly. Not many people have learned to build a successful real estate business and consistently bring others along with them. I won't say that it's been a cakewalk, though. I had to learn how to bootstrap in real estate and put one step in front of the other until I reached the success I have today. But I could not have done it alone. I have a healthy family that allows me the opportunity to spend late nights and early mornings building our family legacy and wealth. Isn't that what it's all about? The finances I make today are to secure a solid future for my family and to create a solid legacy of helping more people obtain wealth.

Before I get to into the details, I will quickly answer another burning question that I know is on your mind: *What makes me qualified to write this book?* Well, besides having made over $1 million dollars annually for the past few years, I also have over 200 real estate deals and six multi-million-dollar businesses. Additionally, I have one of the fastest-growing Real Estate YouTube channels. So in other words, I don't just talk the talk. I walk it. I also earned a bachelor's degree from the University of Connecticut, and I have two masters degrees: one in Economic Development from Penn State, and the other is a Master's in Business Administration

(MBA) from Baylor University. I mention this not to brag, but to let you know that I really know business. I'm not some scam artist trying to tell you things I know nothing about. Most importantly, I'm qualified to write this book because I've been *flat broke*. I've lived in a one-bedroom bed-bug infested apartment with my husband and kids, and I know what it means to hit rock-bottom.

After I reached what I considered success I decided to teach others, and that's what I am doing today. For the past three years I have been perfecting my skills in real estate. Throughout those years, I have personally helped hundreds of my students achieve massive success, while offering tips through my YouTube channel to over 200,000 engaged subscribers. I'll be sharing those very techniques throughout this book.

After our time together, I am expecting you to be convinced that you can have the same success I have achieved if not more. I am expecting you to understand what it takes to move forward and learn clear steps about how it can be done. I also expect you to pivot full force and pursue real estate as a business and not just a part-time hustle.

Now that I have given you my *why*, let me say this. What you won't find in this book is a lot of unproven techniques and fluff. You won't find outdated strategies that no longer apply to today's markets. You won't find things that I have not personally tried and succeeded at. I am going to tell you what I know to be proven techniques. Using this information will give you the foundation for your success.

I believe you will be successful once you set your mind to it and when your goals and actions align. 89% of all millionaires were created through real estate, and it's still the best way to obtain wealth. With such a high success rate, the odds are in your favor. As you continue reading, I want you to keep an open mind and approach each chapter without any preconceived ideas. When you approach this book with an open mind and follow the blueprint, you will have success. The more open you are to the concepts and information, the more success you will receive.

Are you ready? Let's dive in.

Get your free Real Estate Training today.
Visit: www.noellesfreetraining.com

Chapter 1

LAYING THE FOUNDATION

> *"The best investment on Earth is Earth."*
> —Louis Glickman

CAN YOU SEE YOURSELF becoming a real estate millionaire? I hope you can! It is my desire that as you read through these pages, you will be challenged to reach the level of success—millionaire status—I have been able to attain and maintain. There is an abundance of money to be made in real estate, and quite honestly, I believe it will always be one of the most lucrative and safe ways to create wealth. There will always be a need for real estate because people will always need a roof over their heads. I entered the real estate world with little knowledge, and yet, I had a burning passion to win. I wasn't always successful at it, but I was determined to never give up.

If you have attended any of my seminars or have been following me on my social media or my YouTube page, you most likely know my story. For those who don't know me, no worries. I am going to catch you up to speed! I am not a "typical" real estate guru. In the past, real estate has been dominated by males; obviously, I'm not a male. I am a wife, a mother of five and someone who loves to give back to my community. I am also someone who wants to see everyone win. I am a family woman with a knack for business and creating resources. I have been married to my husband for over ten years, and we have withstood some really hard times. Together we are raising our little tribe of future leaders and CEOs. I can now say that I am so eternally grateful for everything that I have been blessed with. You are now a part of my vision to impact women and men all over the world, helping them unlock the giant within them. I am walking in my purpose, doing what I can to help enlighten those who are looking for a way to bring hope and healing to their families. I know what it means to dream and be frustrated, wondering why things aren't working out like you had planned. I get it, and I understand where you may be today.

Although I have been blessed with material possessions, I will never forget my mission to help restore families and bring them to the awareness of how wonderful their lives can be once they break free from old mindsets, values that no longer serve them, and the fears of what others will say about them on their path to success. Success is a process. I have coached people from all walks of life. Some of my students work in corporate America, others are successful CEOs and others work as minimum wage-earning employees. It doesn't matter where you come from or what your past experiences are. We all ultimately want the same thing in life. And I believe there are no limits to where real estate can take you. Honestly, you don't need any fancy degree to achieve success. It just takes the right mindset, the ability to be coachable, and the passion and commitment to do the work.

My Story

Ten years ago, I was basically broke. I had every type of debt you can name. I had over $100,000 in student loans, two car loans, credit cards of every kind, dental payment plans, payday loans, title loans, and personal loans from strip mall stores. Yes, if there was a type of loan being offered, I applied for it. I worked full-time, and my husband worked full-time as well. But like many Americans, we still lived paycheck to paycheck. I worked to pay bills and paying bills was my entire life. I racked up debt like it was going out of style.

After working my fingers to the bone at a boring corporate job, then picking up a second job during the

Christmas season, trying to sell "It Works" on the side, I did whatever it took to show my family that I was able to take care of myself. I hated asking people to borrow money. Maybe you can relate.

So, what did I do? Well, I started a company. I built it to over 100 employees. It went public, and then I sold it and became an instant millionaire.

Ha!! Yeah right! Just making sure you're paying attention.

That's not how it went at all. Sadly, I just kept on that treadmill until I couldn't take it anymore. One day the inner frustration took a toll on me, and there I stood naked in front of my mirror, dripping wet, crying uncontrollably. I remember falling to the floor sobbing like a baby, wondering why my life was in such a mess. I can still feel the cold tile on my warm bare skin.

That day will be forever etched in my memory. It was the day before we were to be evicted from our home. I had been defeated. With nowhere to turn, I thought about the one option I had if I stood any chance of saving my family from financial ruin. Thinking about it caused me to cringe in fear. I needed to call my great aunt, the only person in our family with any money, to borrow $5,200 to save our house from foreclosure. I had never experienced that level of defeat before in my life and I was devastated. I was used to winning, and for the first time in my life I felt as if my world was caving in. I laugh now when I think about how I had been wired for success and competition at such a young age. If there was a selling competition at school, I was determined to take home the prize. But this time, I had to face the music. *Noelle had failed.*

I swallowed my pride, picked up the phone and called. As the phone rang, my heart pounded through my chest. So many thoughts ran through my head. *How would she respond? Would she hang up in my face? Would she loan me the money but secretly feel like she had power over me? Would she conveniently bring it up in front of everyone at Thanksgiving dinner?* Those dreadful thoughts filled my head. The thought of it all made me cry harder.

To my surprise, the call didn't go as I expected. My great aunt gave me the speech that changed my life forever. She refused to lend me the money to stop the foreclosure. We lost the house, and I was devastated. But afterward, my aunt mailed me a check for the full amount 30 days later. Enclosed with the check was a short letter that told me that I needed to stop living paycheck to paycheck and begin investing in myself. In order for me to cash the check, my aunt required that I spend the money investing in myself. The stipulation was that I could not use the money to pay any bill or creditor. The condition was clear and there was no way I was going to lose out on $5,200.

I had heard about the success people were having in real estate, and with a degree in Urban Planning I had some knowledge about the market. Out of desperation and the need to find some extra money to help pay the bills of a growing family, I used real estate as an additional revenue source. But I didn't want to go all in until I first learned the ins and outs about the business.

The best decision I ever made was to take the $5,200 she gave me to hire a real estate coach. I can say that hiring my coach changed the trajectory of my life undoubtedly. Not only did he teach me the ropes and keep me accountable for taking action, but he did something even better. He turned me on to the world of self-improvement and mindset mastery, which finally helped me to start taking responsibility for myself. Remember that pep talk on the wealth mindset we had in the introduction? If you can imagine those concepts on steroids, you can get a glimpse of how my life shifted. Going from barely scraping by to holding everything down for a few years, to losing it all... Having to start all over again, being embarrassed, and begging family members for money had such a negative effect on my subconscious. Eventually, I began to think that maybe the wealthy life of freedom was something I would never experience. Maybe, I had lost my gusto, and I would be stuck in the corporate world, grinding hard with little satisfaction. My physical reality and fears started affecting my decision-making at a core level. Those fears started to speak louder and louder until eventually I had to decide to shut them down.

To play it safe, I started flipping houses as a side hustle while I still worked my full-time job as a Mortgage Broker. Although I was passionate, I didn't have the blueprint and quickly learned that I was just doing everything all wrong. I overpaid for properties and was over-leveraged—my mortgage was almost the value of the property. I was doing the opposite of building a thriving real estate business. But even with my mistakes, real estate was forgiving. It gave me room to grow and learn. That's how I arrived at where I am today.

I have come to terms that it is not hard to make money in real estate. Even when you make mistakes, you can still make a profit. But if you really want to reach millionaire status, you need a plan, a system, and you need to reinvest. If you want to create recurring revenue consistently, you can't just wing it and hope you luckily strike it rich. There's really a strategic way to make millions, but I didn't know any of that when I started. Had I known this sooner I could have saved myself the embarrassment of losing everything.

In 2008, I filed for bankruptcy with multiple foreclosures, and it was a total disaster. My husband and I ended up moving into my parents' basement with our kids because we had lost everything. I was embarrassed,

I was ashamed, I was scared, and I was disappointed in myself. I have always been a person that takes pride in high achievement, and somehow, I felt I had let my family down. I don't know if you have ever been in a place where everything seems to be riding on your shoulders and you miss the mark, but I can tell you that it's not a good feeling.

> *I was probably the last person people would think would end up buying and selling over $20+ million in real estate before the age of 34, but I did.*

Are you Ready for Change?

I knew I had to make a change. It's as if one day you look up and you realize that after all of the hard work you've done, you really are just running on a treadmill, never really getting ahead and surely not getting rich. That's how I felt when I began this journey. This is also the story I hear from many of my students. They are tired of the hustle of life with no tangible results. They're tired of failing over and over again. But they're also afraid at first, fearful that they may not be successful in real estate. All too often we want to quit our jobs and jump headfirst into the real estate business with the noblest of goals and loftiest aspirations, only to stop and think, *This is just too much. I should just keep doing what I'm doing, stop eating out so much and put a little extra aside in my 401k for retirement.* We just talk ourselves out of living our best lives.

It happens over and over again.

I am sure this isn't the first time you've decided you wanted to achieve financial freedom. Maybe you tried getting a side gig selling Mary Kay, Scentsy, or Herbalife to make a few extra bucks. Or maybe you started your own business on the side, and you think that's really the best way to do it—just keep working for someone else and have a side-hustle —but you still haven't really figured out how to start enjoying the wealthy lifestyle you thought you were after. And all you can think is, *There must be a better way...*

Why I Wrote This Book

I wrote this book for the person who is sick and tired of where they are in life, for the person who is so fed up with never having enough money in the bank and being broke in-between paydays. I wrote this for the person who is feeling uncertain about their financial future and where they will be in a few years. I wrote this for the person who is seeking change and who is ready to push past their fears.

Can I ask you a question? Are you frustrated while working for others? Do you want to be your own boss and make a substantial living using your own gifts and talents, but you don't know how? Are you tired of making others rich while you see little payoff in your paycheck? I know how you feel because I was stuck there for many years. My success in corporate America did not translate into me living the life I knew I was predestined to live. It didn't allow me the freedom to be a wife and a mother. After long hours in the office, I struggled with the guilt of knowing that I was missing out on important moments in my kids' lives. I wanted fulfillment in my life and my family needed me.

This book will be so especially important for you. Did you know that real estate is the first way toward wealth? Ask the 89% of millionaires who generated their income from real estate. And if you think that they all had money in the bank when they began, you are wrong. You may have money, you may have no money, maybe a savings plan, or a 401k plan, inheritance or whatever—it doesn't matter. Real estate gives everyone an equal playing field. We all enter at a different financial status; however in real estate it is less about your net worth and more about using what you have or what you can create to become successful. Real estate can create that for you out of nothingness.

During your journey of success, I will be there for you no matter where you are today. I want to help you finally understand how to make money. I will help you become a millionaire if you follow what I have laid out for you. I am offering you a thorough game plan that will stretch you. In this book we'll be looking at the top ways to start as a successful real estate investor. And I'll be sharing with you the secrets behind what works and what doesn't. I'll show you how you can build a 7-figure real estate business using a combination of wholesaling deals, flipping properties, rental properties, and more. There are a million ways to make a million dollars in real estate, and once you get your feet wet, you will decide which of those methods are suitable for your life and lifestyle.

Lastly, I wrote this book to help you understand that being a millionaire in real estate is about solving people's real estate problems. The more you help others by bringing them *real* solutions, the more profit you'll make. Learning this was a major light bulb moment for me. Instead of chasing the bottom line, I started asking, "Who can I help today?" Jim Rohn says in *My Philosophy for Successful Living,*

"If you help enough people get what they want, you can have everything you want."

This is a mantra I live by, and I truly believe this is why I have obtained the success I have today. I simply started looking for more people to help. I want you to keep this in mind as you pursue your investing business. If you enter this business with the mentality that you are just out for yourself, you won't last long.

Shift Happens!

Let's have a heart-to-heart talk before I load you with great information. As I have already mentioned, you are going to learn a lot while reading this book. Even still, all the knowledge will do you no good if you don't first shift your mindset and open yourself to the idea that abundance is your birthright. You need to understand what that means for you. The ideas of a poverty mentality will keep you from receiving the information in this book.

I remember how difficult it was for me to change my mindset about wealth. I would go to work day after day, week after week, and the financial needle was hardly budging. And to make matters worse, each year I was making more than the previous year, and I still never had any extra money. What a joke! I knew there had to be more to life than the typical rat race so many people get caught up in and never escape. It took me a few years of living in that toxic cycle, but I finally realized I needed to do something different. My job was not going to make me rich; it just wasn't. The bottom line is that when you work for someone else you are just making them money, plain and simple. They let you trade your labor for wages, but they are not in the business of making their employees rich. That's the game. If you don't believe it, then you should put this book down right now, because that is the brutal truth.

Another lie that many people believe is that you can be safe by saving your money and retire with a comfortable nest egg. Trust me, you cannot get rich by saving money. You must first earn more money! With the cost of living rising every year, you will never be able to increase your wealth unless you invest it.

Now that we have established that working a job each day will not get you rich, and neither is trying to sit on your golden nest, let's talk about what will get you rich. The answer is simple. First, you have to want to be a millionaire. I know that sounds crazy. You are probably thinking, *Of course I want to be rich! Who doesn't?* So, let's go into that.

I meet so many people that tell me they want to be rich. But when we get into it, they really don't think they can possibly be rich. They don't believe they can. They don't believe they deserve it. They just don't believe it can happen. I'm always so disappointed because I know that they can. I know that *anyone* can be rich. Anyone can be a millionaire. Yes, anyone. But I sympathize because I used to be the same way. I didn't think it would happen for me. I wanted to be rich, but I also had silly conflicting thoughts like, *Rich people are born.* I thought rich people had advantages I didn't have. Even worse, I thought, wealthy people were against me, and they wanted to keep little people like me down. It was basically just a bunch of foolishness. But it was what I thought.

It wasn't until I made up my mind to become a millionaire that things changed. I remember the day. I was listening to motivational speeches by Earl Nightingale, Bob Proctor, and Eric Thomas. And I remember hearing these words: "All that is required to be rich is a decision." In other words, once you decide you want to be rich, you will be rich. That's it, that's the big secret. Just make a decision. *Pretty simple, huh?*

A crucial step to becoming a millionaire is to shift your mindset to your greatness station. You must elevate your mindset to understand and accept that you can become a millionaire when you decide to do so. Before you see it in the physical state, you must first believe and accept that you already are wealthy. I have learned the principle that whatever you think and truly believe, it will come to pass. My first million dollars was made after I shifted my thoughts, took my personal development seriously, and started hanging around people that had achieved the lifestyle I wanted to live. When you live your life with an abundance mindset, you will find that the things that you have been seeking have been seeking you. It's true!

Recently, I posted a YouTube video on my channel where my husband and I spoke candidly about the financial setbacks we experienced. Our mindset kept us in recurring toxic cycles—even when we would win, it would only be temporary because, in the back of our minds, we kept waiting for the roof to cave it. Guess what? It did. Until I learned and applied the principles and blueprint that I will be sharing throughout this book, I experienced little success. I realized and accepted that the shift had to first start from within, and that was when I saw success in my bank account.

Before we go any further, I want you to set your intentions and see yourself as a wealth-building-attraction magnet that flows with the currency of money instead of against it. I want you to see yourself attracting everything good in your life. See yourself winning despite the losses and setbacks you have experienced. See yourself with millions in the bank and contributing to the people and causes that matter most to you. I want you to see yourself on top. This may be difficult for some, especially if everything around you, including your bank account, is screaming otherwise. This is where your focus must kick in. This is where you must silence the noise and the naysayers. No matter what it looks like today, you must focus on where you are going and not on where you are right now.

I am sure you are saying, "Noelle, what does this have to do with real estate? I thought I was going to learn how to flip and wholesale properties?" Don't worry; we'll get to all of that. Before you learn about real estate, let's first deal with the real estate of your mind, the place where your true net worth resides. In order to dive into the properties and the "real" trading, you must have a clear understanding of what is to follow. To understand real estate or, as a matter of fact, any notion in life, you have to be a great observer first, a genuine learner next, and an avid practitioner last. How can you understand real estate? By keeping yourself connected and learning from coaches and mentors who know more than you do, who have *"been there and have done that."*

Having knowledge alone won't make you a success. I have witnessed many people fail in real estate even after giving them the exact blueprint to win because they couldn't surpass the limiting beliefs in their mindsets, which ultimately led them to tap out. They struggled in the lane of excuses, rejection, self-sabotage, and toxic thinking. When they wanted to move forward, they just couldn't because they were affected by doubt and unbelief. As much as I wanted to help them, I couldn't. Because winning starts from within, and no matter what I did to encourage them and lead by example, I was limited since they spent more time talking themselves out of success instead of working toward their goals and moving forward with perseverance and tenacity. I don't want this to be your story. It doesn't have to be.

As you learn the business and grow into a real estate mogul, I want you to consider me not only as your real estate coach but also as your success coach. To achieve what I have over the past few years you have to use what I have learned and taught myself. You, too, have to think like a wealthy person and use that mindset to get ahead in your career as a real estate investor.

Real Estate Key Terms & Definitions

On your real estate journey there will be some key terms you will need to familiarize yourself with. Before we dive in, I want to share these with you as I will be using these words throughout this book. Make sure you keep this list handy.

Real estate: Can refer to personal or commercial properties and/or land. This includes houses, condos, townhomes, vacant lots, commercial buildings or strip malls, apartment buildings, AirBnBs.

Wholesaling: This is when you find a property that is discounted in price, and then look for an investor to sell the property to.

Fix and Flipping: The act of taking a property that needs renovations or repairs, adding value through those repairs or renovations, and then selling it at a higher price.

Appreciation: Is real estate or any investment that goes up in value. One good example is land, with time the value increases.

Deal Compounding: Taking one deal and using that deal to get another deal. Or using the profits from one deal to fund another deal.

O.P.M.: Other People's Money. This means you use other peoples' money to invest. With cash investors, they receive either a percentage of the return on the real estate deal or interest with repayment.

Residual Income: Also known as passive income. This is money that is paid to you residually. Income can be received daily, weekly, monthly or quarterly. This income is not just a lump sum of money, but income that is received over time.

Chapter Recap

- There is an abundance of money to be made in real estate, and it will always be one of the most lucrative and safest ways to create wealth.

- There will always be a need for real estate because people will always need a roof over their heads.

- A crucial step to becoming a millionaire is to shift your mindset to your greatness station. You must elevate your mindset to understand and accept that you can become a millionaire.

- Set your intentions and see yourself as a wealth-building attraction magnet that flows with the currency of money instead of against it.

- Having knowledge alone won't make you a success.

Notes:

_____

_____

_____

_____

_____

Chapter 2

DISPELLING THE MYTHS

> *"The wise young man or wage earner of today invests his money in real estate."*
>
> —*Andrew Carnegie*

ID YOU KNOW THAT the real estate business is a multi-billion dollar a year business? Yes, you read that correctly. I make hundreds of thousands of dollars in just a few months by investing in real estate. I know just how successful one can be in this business. I also know that many skeptics will try to talk you out of your success. Most times, the negative remarks will come from those who have tried and failed or those who have never tried but are always willing to offer up their unmerited opinion. This is why you have to be so careful about who you listen to. If I had believed the lies about too many people investing in real estate, I would have kept these secrets to myself. There are still many millionaires created through real estate today—this business is an ever-growing business, and it's growing every day. There are too many real estate deals for me to handle by myself, so I know for a fact that there is room for more people to get rich. I am committed to showing you how.

In this chapter, we will discuss the basics of real estate for the beginner. This may be new information for you, or it may be a refresher. Either way, I believe the information is pertinent. You should be able to reference this book as a quick guide as you begin navigating your journey in real estate investing. I truly believe that before you run, you must walk; and before you walk, you must crawl. This is exactly how I want to begin with you. This book includes all the information you need. It includes websites, books and anything that will help you evade the "newbie traps" most beginners often fall into when starting with real estate. I am going to save you mentally and financially from draining your bank account and help you avoid the mistakes that eat your profit. I am going to give you the tools to succeed.

What Are Your Goals?

When it comes to real estate, one of the things we need to talk about first is setting your investor goals. When you start investing, you need to know why you are doing what you're doing. Real estate is still the number one way to wealth. And it's a great time to start buying real estate if you have the purpose in mind, and if you are looking to grow your personal wealth. Having a sure plan will keep you focused. Having a plan will increase your chances of succeeding.

When thinking about your real estate goals, I want you to think about the questions below:

Why are you buying real estate?
Do you want to buy it for the income?
Do you want to use it for growing your wealth?

Answering these types of questions should help you define your goals. Once you know them, it will make a significant difference in your investing decisions.

Most people buy real estate to make money. That's probably one of your goals, right? I can almost bet that you are reading this book so you can make money in real estate. Because of that reason, you have to think differently when making that goal. You can't think like a civilian, but you should think from an angle of a real estate investor. Is there such a way of thinking? There sure is.

It's important that you establish your real estate goals early on. Keep them in mind as a constant reminder of why you started and why you will keep going. This mindset will help you fight off your own doubts and the doubts of others.

Can you become successful in real estate?

Before we start cracking our formula, we must address the white elephant in the room. There's so much misinformation floating around, and I want you to know some myths that you might come across that could sadly act as a barrier for you to take your first step.

Allow me to dispel these myths and quench the fears by helping you tackle the world of real estate. Any new start may seem intimidating at first. However, once you break the major goal into attainable bits and chunks, you'll realize it's a lot easier than you think. You may have heard some horror stories about real estate, or you may have had your own moments of wanting to run for the hills. I want you to unlearn the old lies and learn the right ways to do things.

Myth 1: Real Estate Investing is Hard

This myth may not shock you. You may have heard of it at some point in time. You may have heard it from someone or maybe just felt this way personally. When you enter into real estate investing, you will encounter people who will act as depressants. These people will try to stop you and fill your mind with the struggles you will face when starting. They will try to put into your brain the fear of rejection and tell you that every client is a potential enemy for you. People will try and convince you that you have to struggle, cold call people and complete difficult tasks. They will make you feel as if everyone you talk to is going to reject you or see you as the enemy.

You may have heard someone say these unnecessarily negative words before or at worst, you may have even felt this way yourself. But all of these are completely untrue.

Of course, if you approach potential clients without building a rapport, you could receive an unwelcoming response. This is business 101. You shouldn't expect to pick up the phone and land a prospect without first understanding their needs and offering a solution. This is not to say everyone will welcome you with open arms, even after the warm introduction. There will be a small percentage of those who will reject your help, but you shouldn't allow that to discourage you. Amidst the rejection, there is acceptance. From whom? From the right clients. Trust me, people "need" your help in handling their property. You just need to identify them. Over the past years, I have clients who are happy to receive my call and ask for help.

Let me add this. If you just start cold calling people, or if you start diving for dollars, trying to find vacant homes and skip tracing strangers, you will most likely receive negative feedback. Think about it. Do you want strangers calling and harassing you? Of course not! However, the good news is the right people actually want and *need* your help with their property. And you can make a lot of money while helping others. Of course, there is a method to this, so keep reading.

The second reaction you will receive from other people is skepticism. People will tell you that you don't have the money or skills to invest in real estate. They will tell you about some random person who had a few rental properties and how the tenants destroyed the house, causing the person to lose all their money. Or maybe, they will tell you how the business is dominated by men and it's a good ole' boy business and that you can't get into it without the connections. All of this is untrue!

Myth 2: You Need Money to Start Investing

This is a major myth as it contains the money factor. Remember my story? When I started, I was living in my parents' basement. They didn't encourage my real estate. In fact, they kept telling me to get a "real" job. So, if someone like me can start from bankruptcy, you too can have an equal chance of making it *big*. There are tons of ways to invest, even with bad credit or just no money. So, let's throw this myth into the corner where it belongs.

Myth 3: Real Estate is for the Rich

This is absolutely false. I actually believe that more poor people should invest in real estate so that they can become rich. People think that you need to be a millionaire to start investing in real estate, but it's the other way around. Real estate creates millionaires because, through real estate, you amass properties, income, and assets.

Myth #4: Telling Your Story is Detrimental

I discovered one of the great secrets of really making money in real estate was using my real story to connect and help people with their property problems. My coach taught me the power in my story and showed me that was where my opportunity resided. When I thought about it, telling people about my own foreclosure and the events that followed was something that I thought would make people run for their lives. At some point, I tried to conceal that part of the story and refused to disclose it. I thought telling people about my bankruptcy would maybe make them trust me less. At first, I did not believe him, but opening up and being vulnerable was what people needed to hear to make them feel more connected to me. My tragedy became my greatest treasure in securing clients.

I utilized my personal struggle with foreclosure and bankruptcy and connected with others who had similar issues. I started prospecting to potential sellers who were in foreclosure and those who were behind on their mortgage payments. I started to pick up properties for pennies on the dollars. I was able to connect them with investors who could catch those mortgage payments up for them, and in the end they didn't lose their home. They were actually able to sell it to someone who could pay for it, and at the same time, they did not go through foreclosure, they did not ruin their credit, and they did not suffer the embarrassment of being kicked out of their home by the sheriff.

This was an amazing wake-up call for me. Who knew that I could take my tragedy and my story of losing everything and turn that into a connection tool while helping others? This is how I was able to secure many deals. I was able to relate with them so well and explain to them what would happen during a foreclosure so they could avoid the avoidable and do something better than what I did. I became a trusted resource. I showed them there were options, something I wished I would have had for myself. And in the process, I was earning in two fashions. First, I was earning by picking up my sales commissions from wholesaling; and second, I was earning by helping someone else in the process.

Become a Real Estate Problem Solver

While I was living in my parents' basement, my coach helped me learn all I could about real estate. Because I didn't have any money at the time, he started me off investing in wholesaling without using my credit and without using any of my money. The best advice he gave me helped me to create quick revenue once I applied it. I want to share this with you also because it was a turning point in my business. He taught me how to target and market to people who were having property problems. This is the beginning point for any investor and one you will use as a seasoned investor as well.

The first thing you want to do when you start investing in real estate as a beginner is to be a problem solver. You can solve any property problem by finding the right clients in distress. Distressed clients are property owners who are near foreclosures. For me, there was a great opportunity in wholesaling. This is actually great for anyone who does not want to use their own money. My coach taught me the strategy of finding the potential customers who were the right fit—people I could help. Those people included those who were:

- Running behind on their mortgage payments
- Inheriting a house they didn't want
- Relocating and needed to sell their house
- Going through a divorce
- Filing bankruptcy

Did you know that it is easy to locate people with property problems, and you can generally find these people at no cost? That's right. You can get a good lead list or marketing list for free. I am going to tell you a few gold mines that people rarely think about. If you are working with little to no cash for marketing, these sources will be very helpful. It will take you some research time, but I believe it's worth it.

Millionaire Secret #1- Start Your Property Search on the Internet

People in distress are willing to sell you their properties for pennies on the dollar. When you are ready to begin finding your property, you're going to start your search on the internet. This is a great resource to tap into and grab some handsome checks, if used wisely. Websites like Zillow, Craigslist, For Rent by Owner, and For Sale by Owner are filled with motivated sellers.

Millionaire Secret #2- Check Public Records to Find People With Property Problems

In addition, you will find that the information you need is public. If someone is going through bankruptcy, you can go to the bankruptcy court and see who has filed. If someone is going through a divorce, you literally can go to the court and get a list of people going through a divorce and call those people, offering to buy their properties. If someone is behind on their mortgage payments and they're in foreclosure, they'll receive a notice of default. Again, it's right in the court system. When you visit the court's public record, make a list by visiting their websites to gather data. Once you locate someone who needs help selling their property, connect with them and make an offer to buy the property. It's just that simple. When you begin to understand how simple finding customers can be, you'll discover a world waiting for you to solve their property problems. When you shift your mindset to understand that you are helping people, you will see your opportunities expand.

Real estate brings "real" solutions for people with "real" property problems.

Get your free Real Estate Training today.
Visit: www.noellesfreetraining.com

Chapter Recap

- When it comes to real estate, one of the things we need to talk about first is setting your investor goals. When you start investing, you need to know why you are doing what you're doing.

- One of the great secrets of how to really make money in real estate is to use your real story to connect and help people with their property problems.

- The first thing that you want to do when you start investing in real estate as a beginner is to be a problem solver.

- When you are ready to begin finding your property, you're going to begin your search on the internet. Websites like Zillow, Craigslist, For Rent by Owner, and For Sale by Owner are filled with motivated sellers.

Notes:

_____

_____

_____

_____

Chapter 3

ARE YOU READY TO BECOME A REAL ESTATE MILLIONAIRE?

> *"The bottom line to making money in real estate comes down to buying low and selling high."*
>
> —*Anonymous*

A S I PROMISED YOU, it is my goal to help you become a millionaire in real estate. But what does this mean exactly? Well, you can become a documented millionaire either in liquid cash (the money you have in the bank) or by the real value of your real estate portfolio. I'm a certified millionaire. I don't say I'm a millionaire because I have $1 million in liquid cash. In fact, that is not something that I think anybody really should do unless you're a billionaire or you have hundreds of millions of dollars. Because I am an active investor, I don't keep that much liquid cash by choice. As I earn money, I am constantly reinvesting that to buy real estate continually.

I want to quickly discuss the ways you can identify a millionaire in real estate. We have already discussed liquid cash. Now let's discuss building your personal net worth. I am a big advocate of building your net worth. I have been able to do this through real estate and I know first-hand how this works. Now, just because you own a million dollars in properties, that doesn't automatically classify you as a millionaire. To figure out your true net worth, you need to deduct your liabilities (mortgage) from your assets (real estate).

Assets-Liabilities=Net Worth

Let me give you a quick example of what I mean. Let's say your real estate portfolio consists of five properties. And for the sake of this example, all five of those properties are worth $200,000. If you total them up, you will then be a millionaire, right? Well, not quite. If you don't own all five of those properties outright, then, no, you are not a millionaire. If you have a mortgage of $100,000 on each of them, then, of course, you would be worth half a million, which is still pretty good. That is what your net worth would be. However, if you owned them outright, or if the properties were worth $400,000, and you only owe $200,000, then you would be a millionaire.

Become a Real Estate Millionaire

So, let's dig deeper into how you can become a millionaire based on the definition we just discussed above. Did you know that you can quickly buy five or six properties and have a personal net worth of a million dollars? It's actually not as hard as people think it is. Looking at our example above, you can see how easy it can be.

Example: 5 x $200,000= $1,000,000 (millionaire)

Don't let this number intimidate you. I know you're probably saying, "Well, Noelle, you make it sound easy, but where will I get the money to buy the properties?"

If you don't have the capital to buy a million dollars' worth of properties, like most people don't, I suggest you refer to the wholesaling chapter (Chp. 4) and the business funding (Chp. 11) chapters. Buying properties is not hard. Trust me.

Millionaire Secret #3: Determine Your Niches

Earning your millions in real estate will be easier once you figure out your niches. In other words, determine what type of people you are going to help. At the beginning of your real estate journey, I want you to ask yourself about the type of real estate you want to work with to make money. Be it selling or buying. There are just so many different areas in real estate you can make money. Without the proper knowledge, people will try to put their eggs all in one basket, only to realize later that they have had very little success.

When beginning in real estate, I encourage my students to allow themselves some room for learning and implementation. I didn't have it all together when I first started; I had to learn to become a student before I moved on to creating profit. Before I filed for bankruptcy, I had been in the real estate business for a very short time. Because I am such a quick-learner and adaptable person, I hastily rolled up my sleeves and decided to jump straight in. I had no strategy or game plan. This was a major mistake.

Real Estate Niches

When I mention the top five real estate niches, I am referring to the type of property problems you may encounter. For example, think divorce, bankruptcy, foreclosure, inherited homes, and landlords. These are examples of niches that should be at the top of your priority list. I would suggest you target the people that already own real estate and aim to acquire real estate from them. You will make a profit this way. Let me point out that these are niches and not necessarily types of property investments. Some people will consider a niche the following: fixing and flipping, wholesaling, and rental properties. These could also be considered niches. It depends on the context you're talking about.

So how does one become a millionaire in real estate? You can do so by utilizing these five methods. Finding below-value properties, diversifying your portfolio, creating residual income, creating consistent cash flow, and appreciating property value. Let's look at each one of these.

Millionaire Secret #4: Find Below-value Properties

As a real estate investor, you do not want to "pay retail" for your properties. You want to avoid the Multiple Listing Service (MLS) at all cost. What you want is to buy properties for a wholesale price. It has been said that the MLS is where dummies go to bid on who will pay the highest price for a house. I made this mistake when I first began. As a real estate investor, you want to pay the lowest amount possible for a property so you can make the maximum profit. The lower the price you pay to buy the house, the more money you can make when you sell the house—plain and simple. Now, you may or may not sell the house immediately and get a lump sum of cash. There are a few other savvier options, but I will get into those later.

To secure properties at a wholesale price, you need to buy them at an auction or tax sale, or you need to find sellers who are willing to sell you the house for a low-price. Now, you may be asking, "Why would anyone sell their house to you for a low price?" Let me tell you why. They want money quickly, as in the cases of a divorce, foreclosure, or bankruptcy. Or maybe they want to sell quickly because the home is a complete mess and needs a ton of repairs, and they can't afford to fix them. There are so many reasons people sell their houses to real estate investors for a wholesale price. I could write an entire book explaining that. You just need to remember this. These motivated sellers are out there, and you can buy their homes with 30%-50% equity on day one.

Finding a property below value will most likely equate to you buying from a person who has a property problem. Think about it. If the property is in great condition, it's in the suburbs, and it's a very nice property, then they're probably not going to sell it for pennies on the dollar. But on the other hand, if you find someone in one of the categories we discussed, someone who is three to four months past due on their property, or someone who is going through a divorce and the spouse is getting an unkept property, then it would be a good property to try and buy. Remember, you're looking for a motivated seller. This is where I found all my opportunities in real estate. I was able to put those properties under contract, help those people out, and create a win-win situation. Then, I would fix those properties up and then sell them for profit. This is, truly, how you get to millionaire status in real estate investing.

Millionaire Secret #5: Diversify Your Portfolio

You can become a real estate millionaire by diversifying your portfolio. In addition to selling your properties, eventually you will want to have a portfolio with rental properties. Yes, it's great to be able to sell properties and make lump sums of cash, but a true real estate investor—one who is going to reach millionaire status— is going to have to keep some of those properties just for a little bit and allow the principle of appreciation to build that value and make money for them.

Millionaire Secret #6: Understand Appreciation and Utilize It

Appreciation is a concept in real estate that is absolutely amazing. Generally speaking, we know that properties increase in value over time—that's a great thing about real estate! When you combine appreciation with finding properties at a discounted price, helping people who are behind on their mortgage payments, fixing the property up, and then selling it or keeping it, now you've put yourself in a whole new income bracket.

Millionaire Secret #7: Create Residual Income

As I have previously mentioned, residual income is extremely vital to building your net worth. Rental properties are a great way to create residual income. Having a healthy portfolio of both long- and short-term rental properties will stimulate your residual income with money paid out to you each week, each month, or each day. The choice is yours on how you can do this. In my rental portfolio, I have tenants who pay daily rates—these are my short-term rentals. I also have long-term renters—those who fulfill long-term month-to-month contracts.

There are so many ways you can create residual income, but the important thing to remember is that you can only create residual income if you have a real estate portfolio. In other words, if you are only wholesaling and selling all of your properties, you will never be able to have residual income. I love residual income; this is the money that I make when I am sleeping. It feels good to see those frequent payments hitting my accounts.

If you decide to fix and flip, I suggest that once you finish fixing and flipping, you start keeping some of those properties and start amassing your rental property portfolio. If you don't want to deal with long-term renters in your properties, you can put your properties on vacation rental sites like Airbnb, Vacation Rental by Owner, HomeAway, TripAdvisor or Booking.com. The lists on the internet are endless. I keep my properties booked 90% of the time, and this is even when other people are having trouble getting theirs booked.

Millionaire Secret #8: Create Consistent Cash Flow

Think about what additional deals you can make to help create cash flow. Let's say you are looking to find real estate at a really good deal, a property that is below market value. This means you're buying it for less than its worth, for example, if it is worth $200,000 and you can get it for $100,000 or $150,000. Once you land a deal like this, you are officially investing in real estate. When you purchase the property for a lower price and sell it for a higher amount, you'll start to see your profits roll in. This applies to all real estate, including residential houses, condos or commercial properties like strip malls.

No matter what you buy, your strategy should always be to *buy low and sell high.* This is called Cash Flow. It is money consistently coming into your bank account. I want you to think about what you can do to create cash flow from your properties. What can you do with your property to make money on a monthly basis? Can you rent it out to tenants? Can you put a business in there? Can you make it an Airbnb? Who are you going to put in the property, or who's going to give you money for that property to create your cash flow? Take some time to create a plan and think about where your revenue will come from. The worst thing you can do is to have a property that is sitting. Whether you have an occupant in the property or not, you'll still have the upkeep of the property and the taxes. You don't want to have a property that drains your account; you want one that actively adds to your bottom line.

Millionaire Secret #9: Take Advantage of Deal Compounding

One of the great things about real estate is that it has appreciation. Generally, when you buy real estate, it is going to increase in value over time. And that alone is one reason why real estate has created more millionaires than any other industry. Let me tell you exactly how I became a real estate investor by taking advantage of deal compounding.

First, I started profiting upwards of $5,000-$10,000 per deal on wholesaling, and I earned a couple of checks.

Next, I took those profits and started fixing and flipping. On these deals I made anywhere from $40,000-$50,000. I earned that much on my first successful flip, and that was the beginning. Once I started doing the fix and flip and picking up those big checks, I was able to fix my bad credit, and I moved into the next phase.

Thirdly, I added rental properties to my portfolio and applied the consistent cash flow and residual income methods I mentioned.

As they say, the rest is history. By adding these niches to my real estate portfolio, I was able to quit my six-figure job. Now I'm a full-time real estate entrepreneur, and I get to do basically whatever the heck I want to do. When you learn how to apply these steps you will strategically build a portfolio of real estate investments, and in most cases, you will obtain properties with no money and without using your own credit. How does that sound? Can you see how quickly you can climb to millionaire status? When you systematically purchase houses using OPM, sell some of them for big lump sums of cash while holding on to others. That will appreciate at ridiculously high rates, and you will have the winning formula. It's this formula that builds wealth faster than any 401K plan that I've ever seen.

Chapter Recap

- You will become a millionaire in real estate by utilizing these five methods.
  - Finding below value properties
  - Diversifying your portfolio
  - Creating residual income
  - Creating consistent cash flow
  - Property appreciation

- As a real estate investor, you do not want to "pay retail" for your properties. Which means you want to avoid the Multiple Listing Service (MLS) at all cost.

- The top five real estate niches include divorce, bankruptcy, foreclosure, inherited homes, and landlords.

- You can become a real estate millionaire by diversifying your portfolio.

- Create residual income by having a healthy portfolio of both long- and short-term rental properties.

Notes:

_____

_____

Chapter 4

START WHOLESALING DEALS

> *"Landlords grow rich in their sleep without working"*
>
> —John Stuart Mill

WHEN YOU FIRST START out investing in real estate, wholesaling is a good place to begin. If you don't have good credit or enough money, wholesaling will be your light at the end of the tunnel. Wholesaling doesn't require you to have good credit. It doesn't require you to have money. As I mentioned repeatedly, this is where I started. I was able to just go in basically and sign my name and say I would buy those properties. My real estate coach helped me if I needed to come up with any money for my deals. I used none of my own money and none of my credit. After the deal would close, I would use the profits and compound it to the next deal. Eventually, I was able to snowball it into a big business.

So, what is wholesaling? Simply put, it is getting a property under contract. For those of you who are learning about wholesaling for the first time, I will go a bit deeper into the explanation to ensure I answer any questions. Real estate wholesaling is based on buying and selling houses very quickly without making any repairs. You then assign the contract to an investor. In its simplest form, wholesaling is controlling an asset at a noteworthy discount (a "wholesale" price); and then you resell it (usually as-is) for a tidy profit to either an investor or end-user. The key is having "equitable interest" in the property, which you typically gain by simply having it under a contract to purchase. Once you've done this, you have the right to market and sell that piece of real estate, as long as you don't actually "sell" before you actually "buy."

Usually, wholesalers either:

- Simply assign their contract to the new end-buyer, step aside and collect an "assignment fee" at closing.

- Do a "double closing" instead. In this process, both transactions are closed on the same day, and they collect the spread in the middle as their profit.

The first step to wholesaling is to locate people who have property problems. When wholesaling, I suggest you market to those who are behind on their mortgage payments. When you can get the property under contract and then flip that contract to an investor, the investor will pay you a fee, which is usually $5,000 or $10,000. There's money to be made doing this because there are a lot of people who are losing their properties to the banks. You can step in and help them out by wholesaling. When people say that wholesaling is dead, I challenge that. I personally buy wholesale deals all the time from my students and other investors. In fact, on one deal I bought, I saw the wholesaler make $26,000. But I didn't care about that. When I fix and flip a property, I make over $40,000.

This is wholesaling in its simplest, most straight-forward form, and it's already an extremely powerful concept all by itself. It's hands-down the best way for most newer investors to get started in the business, and many of us make a full-blown business out of it. But did you also know that there is also a thing known as Virtual Wholesaling? In essence, virtual wholesaling is a term for wholesaling houses in markets outside of your own—outside the market you actually live in. Said another way, it's operating a wholesaling business remotely and doing deals mostly from the comfort of your computer and mobile phone.

Many investors make a great living wholesaling houses "virtually" in other markets, either because they don't prefer their own market for whatever reason or because they're simply scaling out into multiple markets simultaneously. Most virtual wholesalers still have to spend a ton on marketing to pull this off well, and they often require a pretty crackerjack team of "feet on the ground" and virtual assistants to make it really work.

It's a solid approach, but I think you'll see it's just the tip of the iceberg in my profit avalanche. So, are you impressed by this wholesaling method? The next one is going to impress you even more. It's called co-wholesaling!

Co-wholesaling is a term that's becoming more and more popular today. Essentially, it means doing a joint-venture wholesale deal with another wholesaler. And there are actually two different ways you can do this:

Way #1: Match your sweet deal to another wholesaler's sweet buyer

Let me show you how this works. Let's say you have a hot property under contract, but you have no cash buyer. Meanwhile, your buddy has no deal, but he's got a great buyer's list. You ask him to tell his buyers about your deal, and you offer to split the profits with him if he can sell it.

You just sold a property by using your buddy's network. Isn't that exciting and profitable?!

Way #2: Take your sweet cash buyer to another wholesaler's sweet deal

It's the same scenario but reversed. When you take this approach, you already know what your buyer wants, and you go out "shopping" for deals on their behalf. You get to play matchmaker. This is my absolute favorite approach. The bottom line and the terms of this agreement can be tweaked, but that's co-wholesaling in its pure essence.

Sounds like a win-win, right? You both brought something of value to the table that the other doesn't currently have. Marry the two together, and you both get a nice piece of the pie to split between you both. In old times, they used to refer to this as "barter," and guess what? This was the way people made money or assets, and so can you!

This may seem more complicated at first, but it's simple, streamlined, and far easier than you may think. Every real estate property has a story; some stories are good and others, not so much. To get into the mindset of being a millionaire real estate investor, you need to become savvy about solving property problems. There are endless properties and endless problems. I personally have a structured system for every property problem.

Millionaire Secret #10: Assignment of Mortgages

With some properties I use the assignment of mortgages method. This is a very clever and completely legal method to have a property deeded over to you simply by signing your name. In most cases, I have obtained a property through a mortgage assignment, and the seller never got a dime. I've amassed a portfolio worth millions using this one strategy.

Millionaire Secret #11: Partner With the Seller

For properties that are in need of major repair, I've partnered with the seller to sell the property. This requires little risk. How this works is that if a property is in need of repairs, I will pay to have the property repaired. I remember one deal where I invested $9,200 to have a property fixed up to sell. Just 65 days later we sold it, and I received a check for $42,217! These types of deals are happening every day. Again, this is about you becoming creative in solving those property problems. I hope I am beginning to spark those engines, allowing you to see the countless possibilities available for you.

Millionaire Secret #12: Pay Past Due Mortgage Payment

For properties that have been in foreclosure, I have been able to acquire them by simply covering for the past due amount of the mortgage. In one case, I amassed a property with over $89,700 in equity for only $6,022. This amount represented the past due amount owed to the mortgage company. Not bad for about 15 minutes of actual work, is it?

Is this a method you feel you can implement? I know these methods can seem far-fetched, but they really work. I have tried every one of these. Think about what I have been telling you so far. There are people that are waiting for you to solve their property problems. You have to believe you have the solution. As you can see, there is no one-size-fits-all approach to building your portfolio. You will need to learn what works best for you. I am simply helping you get rid of any excuse that will hinder you from reaching your millionaire status.

Now let me go a bit deeper and tell you that there are two things you should know about, and these are *Repair value* and *After-repair value*. Your repair value is the amount of work a property needs. In most cases, repairs are common in each property, so there will always be this amount to consider. The after-repair value is the amount that your property will sell for after it is fixed.

To guide you on your road to wholesaling, I want to give you the steps to follow to ensure a successful deal.

1. Determine the after-repair Value (ARV) by looking at the market price of similar homes. You can do that by going in physically and finding the local

area price of households or just use Zillow, Redfin and Realtor.com to see the prices of such properties and how much they were sold for.

2. Once you find your ARV, multiply by 70% and then subtract from repair value.
3. Calculate the repair costs.
4. Make an offer to the seller.
5. Find a buyer to wholesale your deal.
6. Collect Your $5,000- $10,000 wholesale fee.
7. Rinse and repeat.

WHOLESALING PROCESS FLOWCHART

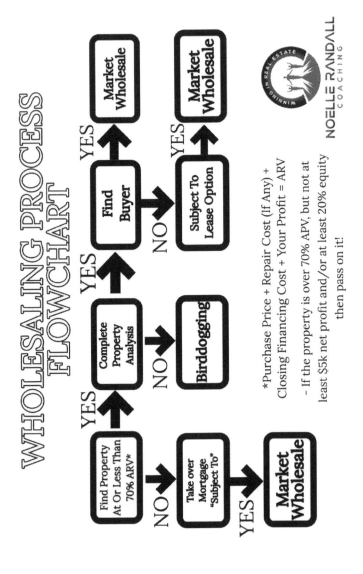

Find Property At Or Less Than 70% ARV* → YES → **Complete Property Analysis** → YES → **Find Buyer** → YES → **Market Wholesale**

Find Property At Or Less Than 70% ARV* → NO → **Take over Mortgage "Subject To"**

Complete Property Analysis → NO → **Birddogging**

Find Buyer → NO → **Subject To Lease Option** → YES → **Market Wholesale**

Take over Mortgage "Subject To" → YES → **Market Wholesale**

*Purchase Price + Repair Cost (If Any) + Closing Financing Cost + Your Profit = ARV

- If the property is over 70% APV, but not at least $5k net profit and/or at least 20% equity then pass on it!

NOELLE RANDALL
COACHING

When it comes down to it, using these methods is how you can really make money in real estate aside from flipping and rentals. Life is full of problems. I can't reiterate this enough: real estate investing is all about solving those problems. The bigger the problem, the bigger your payday! There will be properties you want to keep and others you want to sell immediately. I've made some costly mistakes selling properties I should have held and keeping ones I should have sold. Both can cause you to lose big money. I can systematically, with a simple checklist, determine which properties I should keep and which ones I should let go. It's just the numbers. There are no emotions involved.

Now that you know about wholesaling properties, you are ready to learn how to fix and flip properties.

Chapter Recap
Wholesaling Deals

- Real estate wholesaling is based on buying and selling houses very quickly without making any repairs and assigning the contract to an investor.

- The first step to wholesaling is to locate people that have property problems.

- Assignment of Mortgages is a very clever and completely legal method to having a property deeded over to you simply by signing your name.

Notes:

_____

_____

_____

_____

_____

_____

_____

_____

_____

Chapter 5

ARE YOU READY TO FIX AND FLIP?

> "Buying real estate is not only the best way, the quickest way, the safest way, but the only way to become wealthy."
>
> —Marshall Field

M Y FIRST FLIP WAS a flop! I don't say this to scare you; I tell you this because I want you to be at ease with learning the process. When I began there was so much I didn't know, but with the information I am providing to you, you will not have that problem. One of the biggest mishaps I learned by investing in real estate was that I was fixing and flipping all wrong. When I lost everything by fixing and flipping properties, it was because I was over-leveraged in my properties.

I had too much mortgage, and I had paid too much for them. And when I was fixing and flipping, I was always buying the wrong materials. Either they were too expensive, or they were not expensive enough for the area that we were in. I really did not understand that you must fix and flip a property for the market that you are in. *That's another millionaire investor's secret!*

Once I found my rhythm, there was no stopping me! I went on and on, closing deals and flipping properties. You, too, can do the same. All you need to do is believe and stay focused. Plan, stick to that plan, be appreciative, and stay committed until total execution. The best way to go is to start with a clean slate.

And please stop watching or practicing with HGTV, and those fix it and flip it TV shows. I flip a lot of houses myself, just not in the way those silly shows promote. I usually have to unteach all of the nonsense people learn from those shows. One of the biggest lies being taught is how you get the properties that you plan on flipping.

Most people see those shows and think that if they want to flip a house, they call a local realtor who can help them find a house. Those shows are backed by the National Association of Realtors and those shows are their advertisements. Unfortunately, the simple fact is most real estate agents are not trained in real estate investing—not even a little bit. Therefore, most real estate agents are clueless about working with investors. I've heard about so many people who tried to flip a house that they found with a local realtor in the MLS. This method is fine and dandy if you want to pay full price for a house. But real estate investors have no interest whatsoever in paying full price for a house. Do yourself a favor and unlearn those methods. Utilize the correct steps and make them count for you. Place your ego to the side and be willing to learn the proper way. Start by being a student. If you become a student and are willing to learn, you can become a millionaire in less than a year. Do you want that, or do you prefer to work hard and not smart? I am sure you want to work with little effort and get more return. Who wouldn't, right?

From Wholesaling to Fixing and Flipping

Once you have successfully transacted a few wholesale deals, made your profits between $5,000-$10,000 dollars per deal, and started a rhythm, you are ready to start fixing and flipping. This is yet another easy way to start profiting more considerable lump sums of cash. In fact, the average profit on a fix and flip last year was over $65,000. That's more than what most people make in a year. Imagine if I handed you $65,000 right now. Would you have to go to work tomorrow? Probably not. If you knew how to do this over and over and over, wouldn't that be great? You can even do the same on a low-end house with just six flips a year. One every other month. That's six times $65,000, which equals nearly $400,000. I already did the math because I've done it myself. That's why I'm telling you it's not difficult to do. It doesn't take as much effort as you think. And guess what? There is no barrier stopping you.

Millionaire Secret #13: Avoid Buying Properties at Retail Cost

One of the things my coach shared with me, and which I shared earlier, is, "Only dummies try to find real estate deals in the MLS." The MLS is the database where the properties listed with realtors and real estate brokers are found. If you have ever searched on Zillow or Realtor.com, you will find they pull all their properties from the MLS. In the real estate investing world, we call the MLS the retail marketplace. I am sure you know what an MLS is, but I am reiterating why you shouldn't buy properties there if you want to make any type of profit.

I am also reviewing this with you because I knew to avoid the MLS before I ever tried to flip a house and I still did it and flopped. The bottom line: I didn't listen to my coach, and I bought a home that I found on MLS. I take total responsibility. Although my coach was a great guy and he taught me a lot, he was not an on-going coach that kept holding my hand throughout the process. There were times when I wasn't sure what my next best move should be, and I didn't have a mentor to walk me through it. Basically, he taught me a few things, and we never spoke again. I learned a lot on my own and I fell hard a few times.

Millionaire Secret #14: Follow the Market

Another big mistake I made when I first started fixing and flipping was shopping at Home Depot and Lowe's. I was overpaying for materials and overpaying for labor. I was installing cheaper materials when I should have been installing more expensive things. I installed expensive materials when I should have been using cheaper materials. I really needed to follow the market, but I didn't know this. That is a big mistake that investors make when they are fixing and flipping a property. It's so important to make sure that the materials and the quality that you are using are going to yield the profit that you want to yield.

If you are fixing a high-end property, you're going to need high-end fixtures to get the money out of the property. You're not going to be able to put in cheap Home Depot materials or products in a million-dollar flip. And you surely don't need to put subzero stainless-steel appliances with all the bells and whistles in a $150,000 home in the suburbs. You want to make sure that the materials you're using fit the market and the flip you're doing. You don't want to be in the wrong stores paying retail costs and wasting your money. You really want to be in stores that are designed for contractors, builders, and investors who are actually trying to make a profit with their properties.

MY TESTIMONIAL

By the age of 38 years old I was able to enjoy a low-risk, high-profit real estate investing business that generated around 6-10 quality deals per month for me, at an average profit of $8,000 or so each. This work required only about ten hours of my time each week.

For all of you math geeks out there, that meant my average profit was anywhere from $48K-80K per month. I know it seems like kind of a wide margin to swing, but hey, some months my kids kept me busier than others, and I just couldn't miss one single basketball practice, football scrimmage, or cheer competition. Even the lower-end $48,000 per month provided me a pretty comfortable lifestyle, to say the least.

The Fix and Flip strategy yields big sums of cash when done properly; the keyword is "properly." The problem is there are too many variables that you simply cannot control. Flipping a house is the riskiest strategy of them all, and this is something those house-flipping shows don't tell you. You have to spend a lot to make a lot. You have to find a property with a ton of equity in it and have to figure in the cost and the time for repairs. A lot of things can change before your repairs are complete. Real estate markets can be volatile, and your profits are in jeopardy if the market goes bad.

Millionaire Secret #15: Have the General Contractor Sign an Affidavit

One last piece of advice about flipping houses. Always make the general contractor sign an affidavit stating that all the subcontractors have been paid. The last thing you need is a lien on your title when you sell the house. If you have to pay the lien, then you would have lost twice. You paid the general contractor, and now you are paying it again at closing. Avoid this costly mistake.

My advice to you is to work smart, and that means working on smart deals. If you haven't caught on yet, what you're doing here is building an entire business around marketing so that you can cherry-pick the deals that are the most fun, have the lowest risk, and have the biggest profits. You basically spend 85% of your time, effort, and money (what little money you will spend) on marketing to find sellers who are desperate to sell because they are probably in foreclosure, obtained a property they didn't want from a deceased relative, or they live in a house that is falling apart and the city is about to evict them. In any case, you should market to find them, then they call you, and you use the best strategy to close the deal. Simple.

Completing a Successful Flip

Here is a breakdown of the steps you will need to follow to complete a successful flip.

a. Find a property.
b. Get it under contract.
c. Complete the due diligence.
d. Get funding (private lender or hard-money).
e. Acquire the deal.
f. Oversee the remodeling project.
g. Complete the project.
h. List the home with a Realtor (yes, this is when I recommend a realtor).
i. Close the deal.
j. Get paid.

Flipping can be fun when you know which properties to flip, and they usually come with windfalls of cash. As a real estate investor, you never get attached to a property; it's just a commodity. When flipping a house, keep that in mind and follow these rules:

- Always use OPM (Other People's Money).

- Don't over-improve or do unnecessary repairs or additions.

- Make the home to the standard of your competitors and comparable sales in the area.

- Visit homes in the area and ask the owners to see inside of their homes.

- (I know this sounds weird, but you will thank me when you are not wasting your money putting in granite counter-tops, thereby saving you thousands of dollars and increasing your profits by 22% on average).

- Stay on budget.

- Keep your timeline: For each $5,000 of work, it should be about a week. Ex: $30,000 in total repairs should take about six weeks.

- Stage the home with furniture.

Get your free Real Estate Training today.
Visit: www.noellesfreetraining.com

Chapter Recap

- Avoid buying properties at retail cost.

- You want to make sure that the materials you're using fit the market and the flip that you're doing.

- Always have the general contractor sign an affidavit stating that all of the subcontractors have been paid.

Notes:

_____

_____

_____

_____

_____

_____

_____

_____

_____

_____

_____

Chapter 6

RENTAL BLISS, SLEEPING CASH

> "Real estate cannot be lost or stolen, nor can it be carried away. Purchased with common sense, paid for in full, and managed with reasonable care, it is about the safest investment in the world."
>
> —Franklin D. Roosevelt

S O FAR ON THE journey to real estate millions, you have learned about wholesaling properties and fix and flip properties. Now I want to touch on the topic of rental properties and how you should go about building your rental portfolio. In chapter 2, I mentioned this was vital to becoming a real estate millionaire. I am a big fan of rentals, and I try to talk about it with pure excitement and eagerness. I am going to share with you all there is to know about rental properties and why exactly you should be looking into this. With rental properties there are some traps you need to be aware of. I want to teach you how to buy your first property with no money down. I have lots of rental properties. However, when I first started, I could not afford to qualify for them on my own. Now I love it, and I'm going to show you exactly how to do it so that you can start making money too.

In 2009, after that stint in my parents' basement, I started experimenting with rentals. Eventually, I earned enough money, and I was able to quit my job with just my rental properties. Let me help you get there by starting with your first rental property. And you must be thinking, why would you want a rental property, right? One of the things that I use rental properties for is cash flow income. Each month while the tenant is paying the rent, they are paying down my mortgage. Additionally, I make sure to get properties in the right place. My coach told me about finding properties in a good place, and I am going to do the same for you so that your property values increase or appreciate and not lose value or depreciate.

The short-term rental market was valued at $100 billion in revenue in 2016. It was expected to grow to $167.9 billion in 2019. (VRMA)

Millionaire Secret #16: Sell Tenant-occupied Properties for Maximum Profits

One of the things that I was able to do with my rental properties was to sell the properties while they were tenant-occupied. Think about how amazing of a deal this was for a buyer. I was actually doing them a favor by saving them the hassle of finding a tenant for the home. I love when I can create win-win situations. I landed some big paydays by using this method. I'm talking $40,000, $50,000, and even $100,000 at a time on one property.

This one method has multiple streams of income attached to it. By having someone living in the property, I didn't have to pay the mortgage. I would keep my properties tenant-occupied for a couple of years. By later selling the property, I was able to walk away with a bigger profit. Were you able to follow along with this scenario? Did you see how I earned residual monthly profits on the property? I used the money to pay the mortgage on the home as well as pocket some of the extra money. And then, by selling the home, I was able to walk away with the profits.

This is why I would encourage you to add rental properties to your portfolio. It is not just the monthly revenues you can get, but also those lump sums of cash when you sell your properties. Additionally, you can gift those properties to your children or family members, and you can leverage them by borrowing money against the property. It really opens up a ton of doors for you when you have rental properties.

So, if you are thinking about getting a rental property, get clear on what it is that you want. Know that you want that monthly income coming in as a residual income. Yes, but keep in mind that you can sell those bad boys and start getting six-figure checks. Six-figure checks. Yes, let's get into that part.

Remember the acronym OPM. This is a good place to apply it? Banks have money to lend; hard money lenders have money to lend. There's private money; for example, the person that you are buying the home from in many cases can lend you money or give you equity, and so many different things. Being creative in your financing options will work to your benefit in the long run.

Now I must forewarn you because you need to understand the process so that you don't become over-leveraged. I am saying that you don't want to mortgage all of the value in the equity away on the property. You want to have some equity so that you receive lump sums of cash when you sell the property.

Millionaire Secret #17: The B.R.R.R.R. Strategy

When I mention OPM within the guidelines of rental properties, I'm referencing using a hard money loan in most cases. Let's say the home you are purchasing will need some repairs. You will probably need to find a lender to cover the cost of your repairs. They may not need to cover the entire amount, because maybe you can put in some effort by fixing it up. But in many cases you need to hire a crew to fix it up for you. Once the house is fixed up you can refinance out of that mortgage and then rent it out to a tenant. This is a very popular concept in real estate investing called "BRRRR". As hilarious as it sounds, it means to buy, rehab, rent, refinance and repeat!

Because you have a tenant in the home, and they're paying the mortgage, that rent is considered income. Hard money lenders and the banks will give you credit for the rent your tenant is paying and apply that as future revenue that you're going to bring in, making it easier for you to get qualified for a loan. But don't forget the last step of BRRR: repeat. That is how we build our portfolios and get tons and tons of properties.

The Best Properties with Little Money

When we're talking about how to find these properties, you have to find people with property problems like I told you before, as that is the best approach to achieve success. With the BRRR strategy, which is again just one of the strategies, you can start getting properties with no money. How? By finding people that are in a financially stressful situation, where the property is in distress, and it needs some repairs. But if you fix the property up, it would be worth more.

Apart from the banks, there are tons of lenders called hard money lenders. And then, some private lenders will literally lend you money to buy the property, fix it, and even give you some money so that you have some reserves in case something goes wrong. This all fits in one big strategy of finding people that have a property problem. I know I have been mentioning this again and again, but it is just so important as a concept and as a deal maker. If you don't want to spend a lot of money and don't have a lot of cash lying around, you will need to find people who will lend you the money you need.

Millionaire Secret #18: Where to Find Your Lenders

Finding contacts for lenders is easier than you think. It will take a little effort on your part, but you will probably be surprised how easy it is once you begin your search. I would advise you to first start your research by attending real estate investors' association meetings to start reaching out and finding hard money lenders.

Once the money issue is out of the way, it is time to find the people with property issues. You marry the two issues, and a solution is born. This is the process of acquiring properties with no money of your own. You are literally using someone else's money to generate an income for yourself. Also, there are amazing ways to do that if you marry those two concepts that I just gave you. Let me add a bonus tip on top of all that creamy cake.

Millionaire Secret #19: The "Subject-to" Method

When we find people with property problems, the bonus is that many of them can sell you the property "subject-to." This means the mortgage they have will stay in place. If they're in a situation where they need to sell the property, and they are willing to lease or sell that property to you, that's a good find as well. When you don't have to buy the property, you can lease the property. When they move out of it, you can make money on that property by putting a tenant in there. And don't forget the option of putting that property on Airbnb as I have done. Start thinking about finding people with those property problems and educating yourself on "subject-to" and on how to make lease purchases.

Many of my students are using this invaluable method, and it's how they are getting their rental properties right now. I literally just had a student who found a property in probate, and the owner had no mortgage on the property. They owned it free and clear. The owner had inherited the property from his mom. Now my student has their very first rental property, and they didn't have to come out of pocket with any money.

Millionaire Secret #20: Utilize Crowd-funding

There is a new method that has arrived in the real estate market to offer alternatives for those seeking to buy rental properties using OPM. It is an amazing approach that almost anyone can do. It is known as the "real estate crowd-fund." Another term I use is Joint Venture (JV). I partner with my students by this method, and it is purely scintillating. You too can leverage this amazing method to source your real estate investments. When it comes to crowd-funding, here are two of the main ones. These are Kickstarter (www.kickstarter.com) and truCrowd (*www.trucrowd.com*). It's pretty easy to start a campaign. All you have to do is make a post to begin obtaining investments from investors for as little as $500. You can buy properties from across the country and sell them, splitting the profits as dividends.

You can start one on your own, or if you don't want to fully commit to one of your own, you can invest with mine. Right now, at Nuurez.com, we have over $200,000 in funds for real estate purchases. If you invest in us, you get quarterly distributions. It is a win-win in both cases. Either you become an investor, or you become a crowd-fund initiator. People will invest for you, and when you make profits, you just have to split the payments.

If you want to learn a bit more about rental proper-ties and crowd-funding, you are most welcome to join our free webinars or visit the website for more details. Just visit Nuurez.com and click on "invest." It will take you to our webinars where we talk about crowd-funding, our investments, properties and the distribution of profits. You, too, can do the same once you master the tactics of crowd-funding and can make it your own formula of success. You can learn from us about our own crowd-funding and then maybe try it out before you are ready to start yours. The options are endless; you are your own boss.

Chapter Recap

- One of the things that I was able to do with my rental properties was to sell the properties while it was tenant occupied. This generated maximum profits.

- *Use the* "BRRRR" strategy: buy, rehab, rent, refinance, and repeat!

- I would advise you to first start your research by attending real estate investors' association meetings to start reaching out and finding hard money lenders.

- Start thinking about finding people with those property problems and educating yourself on "subject-to" and on how to make lease purchases.

- Utilize Crowd-funding to help you get the funding you need.

Notes:

_____

_____

_____

_____

Chapter 7

MARKET, CONVERT, SOLVE

> "The major fortunes in America have been made in land."
>
> —John D. Rockefeller

TO BECOME SUCCESSFUL IN real estate, you must find below-market deals from sellers who want to sell their homes. To find these deals you need to become comfortable with the idea of marketing. I know that marketing is not going to be a favorite of yours unless you have experience in it. I'm sure that unless you work in marketing, you probably don't know how to market "properly." Even most marketing people suck at it! Marketing is about testing, and truthfully "testing" ads can get really expensive. Most small investors or business owners don't have a marketing department stacked with cash that they can blow by running radio, television, or internet ads. By the end of the chapter I want you to be comfortable with the idea of marketing, but first let me discuss some affordable and proven methods you can incorporate.

I want to teach you how to make your marketing ads. Now, I know you are thinking that this step is easy-breezy, but trust me. This is the step that can keep you waiting for months for a lead if it's not done right. To connect with potential leads you should create ads that are engaging, that are not too fairytale-sounding. The ads need to be real, just like your story. You have to find a visual and compelling way to connect with the clients. It can be the way you write your typography or the pictures you use. No matter what you choose, be as creative and minimalist as you can be.

Millionaire Secret #21: Identify Your Target Market

Once done with this big step, the next step is to know your target market. With any business, identifying a target market is a must. It's the only factor that can help you create a million-dollar real estate business as I have done. You can have the best ads, but if they are not reaching the right clients, you are wasting time, money, and clientele. So, you have to make sure you do your research first.

Do you remember the court-lists we discussed earlier, and the other ways you can use to find foreclosures, default notices, and bankrupt people? Yes, that! Use that info and target that population to get the best results.

Aside from creating your ads and then finding your target market, there is one more step left. Generating leads. How do you do that? Let's find out how you generate leads.

You have more options than this book can contain. The options are endless and all of them will work like magic if you use the right "words." That's right, words matter! And the place you use them matters even more. What places am I talking about? Well, I am talking about the target market again. For a real estate investor, there are two primary markets: Online (internet) and Offline (your local area) marketing.

Online marketing is pretty easy to do and takes very little time and effort. Websites like Craigslist and Zillow are the go-to options. You can just type "real estate" in your search engine, and you will find hundreds of results. If you want to level-up, you can even build your own WordPress website and start marketing it at an affordable price. Internet marketing is a breeze, and you will know just how easy it is to market yourself.

Offline marketing is key to any real estate investor because, as they say, real estate is local. Offline marketing includes posting "We Buy Houses" signs, direct mailing and finding foreclosure lists. These are inexpensive and very effective methods. The right combination of online and offline marketing will fill your pipeline full of deals worth hundreds of thousands of dollars.

The Easy Way to Connect

There is also another way to connect to potential leads, and that's through mailings. It's very easy. You can mail a letter or a postcard and start targeting people who are behind on their mortgage payments. Let's use an example.

Say they're three months past due, and the mortgage payment is $1,500. That's $4,500 that they are past due, and by now they're going to get what's called a notice of default letter. So, they get this letter in the mail saying they've defaulted their mortgage. Now, not only do they owe the past due amount, but they also owe late charges and fees. For the average person who receives this notice, their first response is to freak out, and most people just resign themselves to the fact that they're going to go into foreclosure. This is the perfect scenario for someone who would be a good potential lead.

You can send them a letter saying "Hey, I can help. I'm a real estate investor, I buy homes for cash, and I'm connected to a big network."

This is not an uncommon scenario, and I have found properties with hundreds of thousands of dollars in equity in them. When the person was getting foreclosed upon, I was able to get those properties for just a few thousand dollars. I could either flip the contract to someone else and make $5,000-$10,000, or I could keep it myself, take those mortgage payments over, and then sell it later, earning all that money.

This is the cornerstone of how you are going to get a portfolio. I literally have students that are picking up five or six properties and becoming millionaires in less than a year just by targeting people that are having an issue with their properties. They seize the opportunity to get them under contract and then flip those properties to another investor or keep them for themselves and then cash in by selling them later.

Now, you have made your ad, posted it on all the marketing channels, and are waiting for your leads, or maybe you're looking for one yourself. Let's say you find one. What do you do or say to them? So, if someone calls you from your advertising, that is the true essence of a lead. It is a very good thing.

If they are calling you, then they have a problem. Real estate investors love problems, and that is how we make money. By we, I am including *you* as well. As an investor you should fall in love with property problems. When your phone rings, you know that it is someone either wanting to sell you their home for a super-low price or someone wanting to buy a house from you for a big profit.

Now, there are some nuances to knowing exactly what to say when your phone rings to get them actually to sell you the house. But through some trial and error, I've got it down pat. They sell me the house, and I make money; it's just that simple.

I've even started letting some of my students use the specific "marketing response" script I've perfected myself as a shortcut. But I digress...

Once you've turned on your marketing, it's like turning on a fire hose. Your phone will ring with people literally wanting to build *your* wealth.

Now, you have started generating leads, and people are calling you each second. What do you do then? It is time to make some noise...Get those sales!

Making the Sale

Now that you've got your phone ringing off the hook with people wanting to buy or sell you a house, we need to get them to sign the contract. In sales, we call this "converting leads."

While this is the hardest part to learn, rest assured as it's still pretty easy. It's way faster and easier compared to how most real estate investors build their portfolios.

Millionaire Secret #22: Classify your Seller and Convert Higher

There will be three types of people you will talk to. When talking to these three personality types, saying the right words is crucial to them taking action and closing the deal with you. The three types are:

- The "numbers" person
- The "gut-feelings" person
- The "over-thinker" person

Let's start with the *numbers person*. The numbers person just wants you to tell them the numbers and go away so they can think about it. They pretty much know they can't afford the house or it needs too many repairs, and they can't afford to fix them, so you are their only option. But still they want to be in control. You have to play their game but flip it so that you get what you want. You will have to give this person the numbers pretty quickly, or you won't stand a chance. The secret is giving them the numbers and then answering each of their rejections in a systematic way. No matter what number you give, they will say it's too low. All you have to do is give them the exact breakdown of how you got to your number and then ask for the contract again. These people just want to know the "why," and you have to give it to them if you want to earn their respect and get them to do business with you.

The second personality type is the *gut-feelings person*. This person is pretty easy to deal with, but they are easily distracted, so you will have to keep them focused. I absolutely love dealing with these people because all you have to do is be "likable" and move fast. You will win the deal every time. This person allows for a pretty swift deal.

Finally, the *over-thinker person* is probably the most common person you will deal with as a real estate investor. These people want to do business, but they just can't seem to make a decision. You have to know the right words to inspire them to take action. It basically comes down to explaining to them that you are their best option.

For example, let's say the person is facing foreclosure. They can sell you the house and their troubles will be over. They can save their credit and move on with their lives. You can win the deal each time by intelligently and patiently going through what foreclosure really does to a person's credit. You can let them know how their wages can be garnished, how they will have terrible credit for ten years, and how the IRS can file a lien on their future property. This is all after their possessions will be thrown out onto their front lawn in front of their neighbors. Now, that is not what any person would want to be done to them, and you can score by stepping in and making them feel safe again. All you have to do is paint the picture, and they will sign the contract. It's like stopping a baby from falling down the stairs.

It took me a little trial and error to figure this one out, but now I've got it down to a science. I can explain exactly why they should sell me their house in less than 60 seconds.

Study the personality types and become familiar with them so you can quickly identify them. By the end of it all, you will be able to determine which of the three personality types you are talking to. They always give you clues based on their answers, and you will know exactly what to say to get them to take action.

Millionaire Secret #23: Pick a Strategy to Close the Deal

The right strategy is what really makes or breaks you as a real estate investor. You will find that it's not that difficult to find people with property problems. You will also find that it won't require any of your own money and very little of your time. So, once your phone is ringing off the hook, and your pipeline is full, the key is going to be what you do with the property.

There are ten primary strategies that you should utilize, and I will gladly share them with you.

1. Fix and Flip
2. Subject-to (Mortgage Assignment)
3. Wrap-around mortgage
4. Wholesaling

5. Short-sale
6. Rental Property
7. New Construction
8. House Swapping
9. Auction
10. Combo-listing

Based on the scenario, you will use one of the above strategies or a combination of two to three strategies. Most people are more than familiar with all the house-flipping shows, and newbie investors flock to this strategy. It's not a bad strategy; I'm not trying to say anything bad about flipping houses.

But as I explained earlier, we get our properties wholesale, and we have three strategies to get properties at wholesale prices. You guessed it, we use our marketing to find motivated sellers who want to sell us their homes quickly for cash.

Millionaire Secret #24: Market, Convert, and Solve (MCS)

Everything I have been referencing in this chapter falls under the MCS. Isn't having a clear strategy and a plan to find your properties 100 times better than calling around unknown numbers and driving miles to find houses? All you need to do is focus on finding people that have property problems. MCS is what I call my "secret formula."

But the thing is, there is no secret information when it comes down to it. Like most systems, my secret formula uses the same basic information that is already readily available and being used by other investors in different ways right now. But they use the strategies in specific ways, for specific situations, for specific outcomes.

And truth be told, we also specifically use many other common activities most investors don't even know about or know how to use. The result is pretty freaking amazing.

Stuff We Don't Do:

With the options I presented to you, you won't have to deal with these issues:

- Expensive marketing campaigns
- Scrounging for deals—you will know exactly how to get the best deals in your town
- Walking into scary, disgusting houses
- Worrying about how much you should pay for a house
- No hassle trying to figure out if you have a "good" contractor or not
- Stressing about if you are being overcharged or about how much something should really cost
- No need to hunt down investor-friendly vendors who actually want to help you make money

Chapter Recap

- *Identify Your Target Market.* With any business, a target market is a must, and it's the only factor that can help you create a million-dollar real estate.

- *Classify your Seller and Convert Higher.* Study the personality types and become familiar with them so you can quickly identify them.

- *Pick a Strategy to Close the Deal.* The right strategy is what really makes or breaks you as a real estate investor.

Notes:

_____

_____

_____

_____

_____

_____

_____

_____

Chapter 8

MILLIONAIRE SECRETS FOR PURCHASING PROPERTIES

> *"A man complained that on his way home to dinner he had every day to pass through that long field of his neighbor's. I advised him to buy it, and it would never seem long again."*
>
> —*Ralph Waldo Emerson*

I GET SO EXCITED TALKING about real estate. Can you tell? In this chapter we will discuss tips for the evaluation and purchasing of properties and helpful information to aid you in evaluating which property is best for you to invest in. Knowing this will help you earn a better return on your investment and save you from bad deals and unnecessary stress.

To be successful as a real estate investor, you must understand how the customer thinks and how you can utilize that information in your favor. To become a millionaire real estate investor, you must put on the customer's shoes and think like them. How do you think like a customer? You become one! Let me help you by providing some trends of consumer purchasing behavior. You will need to follow the market trends and know when a location is hot and when the buying has slowed down. Setting clear goals for your business will help you forecast what you should be doing and when you should be doing it.

Millionaire Secret #25: Don't Purchase Properties During the Hot-selling Months

Do you know the best time to buy properties as a consumer? It's during the summer! That's right. Most of the buyers buy homes during the summer and the spring. There is a reason for that, the winters keep them cozy and stuffed, and they are out on their home-buying sprees when the snow melts away. The spring and summer seasons are the times when most home selling happens. Now you're probably asking, "But would not that huge number of sales create competition?" Yes, it does. And that is why, we as investors usually buy when there is hardly any competition. What does that mean? It means that we don't purchase properties during the hot buying months. These are the months we focus on selling to receive our maximum profits. The lesson to be learned here is to buy when no one is buying and sell when everyone is selling.

Millionaire Secret #26: Properly Evaluate the Property

When evaluating properties, always look at the land value. Most people look at the property. They look at the house and the home improvements, but really it is the land you should be looking at. You want to purchase property in areas in which homes are appreciating. Check to see what the surrounding properties are selling for to compare this.

The property's value is usually based on comparables or the comps, but it's important to consider its key factors. Comparables are similar or recently sold properties of the same nature that agents and appraisers use in determining the value of a property. Comparables can be greatly used to determine the listing price of a property before listing it on the market, enabling a buyer to determine a fair offer price. They will also aid you in knowing the current value and potential equity.

For instance, if a similar property is sold near your potential property and your location is strategically better, your property will be worth more. Some other key factors that can influence a property's value include location, job market, property taxes, and maintenance. Take all of these into consideration when evaluating your potential property.

Location

The most important among the key factors is location. The location is the only thing that can never change. You may opt to improve your property—you can renovate it all you want—but you can never change where it is positioned. If your property is located in a rural area, it will be worthless as compared to those properties found in urban areas.

TIPS FOR PURCHASING PROPERTIES

Millionaire Secret #27: Stay Away from Large Projects That Aren't in Your Area of Specialty

What type of property should you stay away from when you first get started? You should stay away from large projects that are out of your expertise. Unless you are a seasoned investor, I would suggest you stay clear of historic homes. I remember when I tried to flip a historic home and how badly it ended up for me. I was out of my area of expertise, the flip took way longer than I had expected, and it cost me much more capital than I had available. It was the ultimate blow that landed me in my parents' basement. I quickly learned to stay away from the homes that weren't in my area of

specialty. My advice to you is to keep away from renovations that are extremely large, complex, and costly.

Millionaire Secret #28: Stay Away from the Property Other Investors Don't Want

This is actually one I would consider a red flag. If there
is a property that other investors are avoiding, there's
usually a reason why. Pay attention to the property
nobody else wants or the property that is not highly
sought after. If no one else wants it, neither should
you. You must know that when you're a new investor,
older investors will try to dump their least desirable
property on you. They know that newbie investors most
likely don't know what they are talking about and/or
doing. And trust me, it's very easy to spot a new investor,
usually because they're not well educated in the process
and they're asking stupid questions. You want deals that
anybody would want. I am not saying to get into bidding
wars with the competition on the hottest properties, but
I am saying to make sure you aren't the only investor
that thinks a property is a good deal. Do your research.
If the property is hot, others will want it as well.

Millionaire Secret #29: Don't Tie Yourself to the Real Estate

How do you know if you've found a good property?
Remember, it's not about the property; it's about buying

below market value and making a profit. I can care less if the property is a dilapidated mobile home. The only question I want to know is, Can I make money off of it? A true real estate investor is not tied to real estate. They don't care about the real estate. They care about the profits. That's another move a newbie investor will make in error. They start looking at the beauty of the property. They want the house with the white picket fence and new granite countertops, but that's not what they should be focusing on. The only thing you should care about is how much money you can make on the property.

Millionaire Secret #30: Use OPM for Your Investment Purchase

When consumers think of buying a home, taking out a long mortgage usually comes to mind. They will research the best lenders with favorable interest rates. This works for properties that will be lived in for a long period of time. But remember, as an investor you think differently. Your approach should be to never use your own monies or to tie up your liquid cash if at all possible. You need to do what most real estate investors do and buy the property on hard money loans, especially if there is fixing and flipping involved. Now, I am not saying hard money loans are the best way to go all the time, especially if they are private lenders. Depending on the number of investors you have borrowed from and the number of fix and flip property portfolios you have, your investors are likely to run out of money. This mostly happens at the end of the year, so you should be wary of that. As with anything, do your research and make sure the terms fit within your goals. I want you to get in the habit of using OPM to purchase your real estate.

If you are still on the fence about whether or not you can do this, I suggest you dip your feet in the water. The best time to become a real estate investor is now. I have been sharing some very valuable nuggets, and I hope you are able to take it all in.

Chapter Recap

- **Don't Purchase Properties During the Hot-Selling Months.** The lesson to be learned here is to buy when no one is buying and sell when everyone is selling.

- **Properly Evaluate the Property.** When evaluating properties, always look at the land value, not the house nor the home improvements. It is the land you should be looking at.

- **Stay Away from Large Projects That Aren't in Your Area of Specialty.** You should stay away from large projects that are out of your area of expertise.

- **Stay Away from the Property Other Investors Don't Want**

Notes:

_____

_____

_____

_____

_____

_____

_____

Chapter 9

HANDLING YOUR BUSINESS PROPERLY

> "Real estate investing, even on a very small scale,
> remains a tried and true means of building an
> individual's cash flow and wealth."
>
> —Robert Kiyosaki

OKAY, MILLIONAIRE! WE'VE TALKED about how you can evaluate your properties with clear goals and buy them using consumers' shopping trends. So far, you know all there is to know about the types of properties, those to avoid and those that are hot. You also know how to find your leads and the property problems you are solving. Before I send you on your way, I want you to now focus on the business side. It's important that you run your business like a business and not a side hustle. If you operate your real estate investor business as a business, it will pay you like one.

I have listed the steps below to help aid you in the process. By setting up your professional business, you will not only be formally welcoming to your clients, but your return on your investment will be much higher than a person without these valuable additions.

Step #1: Business Registration and Incorporation

Your business registration is the first step to starting off your real estate investor career. I advise you to become a registered business as this protects your personal property and assets from any business litigation. How do you do this? You would need to register with your state with the choice of Limited Liability Company (LLC), S Corp or a C Corp. Do your research to see which corporation type is best for you? If you feel you need more hands-on assistance, you have options like Legal Zoom or a local business attorney.

Step #2: Federal Employer Identification Number

Once you register your business, you should then file for your Employer Identification Number, also known as your EIN. You can do this by visiting irs.gov to have your free EIN generated for you. Doing this is very important because the EIN is equivalent to your business social security number (SSN). But it is not for you; it is for your business. Yes, you will now have two social security numbers assigned to you: your personal and your business numbers. Every business, if it's a legitimate business, should have an EIN number. This is the IRS number that is specific just for you, and it is an important step in separating you from your business. Having an EIN is very important when it comes to obtaining funding and business credit.

Getting this registration may sound like a lengthy process, but trust me, it takes only a few days. I have students who have registered their businesses in a matter of days and began flipping and flapping. In some states, it can literally take some hours due to their online system support. This is not as overwhelming as it may seem.

Step #3: Establish a Professional Online Presence

Once you have completed your registration and received your EIN, it is time for you to create a professional appearance by adding a professional phone number, a professional email and a website to your repertoire.

For emails, you can use Google Suite, Microsoft 365 or any other paid email service that can cater to your needs. For your website, you can have one created by hiring a developer or by using WIX.com or similar platforms, which provide easy-to-setup websites for your business. There are many platforms to find these developers. Platforms like Upwork, Fiverr or even a walk-in software/developer hub can bring you a good bargain for your bucks. All these value additions will make your company stand out and look fortified within the industry. Now, when done with the processes mentioned above, you are all set to head out in the market and make those deals.

Step #4: Funding Your Business

One of the main areas that hinders many businesses from growing is having the capital to start or expand their business. By now I am sure you realize I believe that nothing should hinder you from building your real estate empire, including money. I have been helping my students discover resources that are readily available for anyone willing to do a little work. Did you know there is literally more untapped money for startups than there's ever been in history? Yes, it is true. There's more money for startups, for women-owned businesses, for minority-owned businesses and for veteran-owned businesses. The money is sitting and waiting for you, and I want you to access it.

You can find and secure money for your business regardless of your credit score or your educational background. There are just a few things you need to do to access anywhere from $10,000-$20,000 for your business, in your business's name, in just a matter of weeks—not years or months. The capital options include grants and loans, and some even have forgivable parts to them. This is money you do not need to pay back. There is no shortage or lack of money available; you just have to know where to look.

Here is a golden nugget that many people don't know. You must have a clear plan for your business in order to receive funding. You should not only have a business plan, but most funders want to know what you are going to do with the money once you receive it. My advice to you is to have a plan before you apply for it. Think about it this way. If your child came to you and asked for money and didn't tell you what the money was going to be used for, would you easily give it to them? Probably not. The funders of these grants and loans have the money waiting for those that have a clear course of action and who are prepared. Before you go ahead and start applying for funding, I want you to take the time to be clear about what you're going to do with it.

Let me go a little further to help you understand what they are looking for. Are you going to use the funds for expansion? Are you going to use them for marketing? Are you going to use them to buy equipment? Do you need to buy computers? What will you do with the money? You need to have a business plan already written out. Make the proper preparation to receive this funding.

Millionaire Secret #31: You Will Increase Your Chances of Receiving Funding If You Specify How The Funding Will Be Utilized for Equipment Purchases

Here's another secret that few people know about business funding. One of the things that you want to indicate on your application is that you'll be using the funds to invest in equipment. In other words, you will be utilizing the funding to create additional revenue for the business. In your business plan and application, you'll include any equipment and inventory you're going to purchase, and then you'll disclose how you're going to generate revenue from that purchase. If you just start talking about all of the things you need to have a business or the things you need to even get started, they're not going to give you the money. Funders want to know you will do well with the funds by creating additional revenue and growth opportunities in your business.

Organizations want to invest in winners; they want to invest in people they think will be successful. No one wants to invest or give money or even a grant—they don't even want to give free money—to someone who will not be successful and who will be closing their doors very shortly. So make sure you have a plan for what you're going to do with the money and how it can make you money. Make sure you're really clear.

Millionaire Secret #32: Where to Access Funding for Your Business

If you want to apply for grants, let's discuss where you can find funding opportunities once your business plan is in place. There is a website for grants that I recommend called Grants.gov. Take some time to look at this website. It can be a little bit daunting because it is the government's website for different grants available for all different types of businesses, but it's absolutely free to access. I have students that have received $10,000- $30,000 in grants in the last few months. I have personally received grants, loans and forgivable loans through Grants.gov. If you're a minority, a woman, or you're a disabled veteran, make sure you search for those grants first because they will have a smaller pool of people competing for the grant. You'll be very surprised how few minorities are actually seeking out grants, and there are untapped funds available and waiting. Because you will have a plan for your business, you should go ahead and apply.

The next place you want to look for free money for your business is the National Association of the Self-Employed (NASE.org). They have tons of free money out there for startups and established businesses as well.

Make sure you visit their website and apply for funding at least once per week. They're constantly adding new grants, new loans, and new funding partners. All of this money is available, and tons of it is untapped. Again, literally, there are billions of dollars and untapped funds for your business.

Another great place for money—and this is when you have low credit scores—is a company called ACCION. Their website is accion.org. Accion is a community development institution that lends to startups; they will lend to women-owned businesses and minority-owned businesses. They literally have money set aside just for this purpose—to lend to startups. You don't want to sit on this good information, so go ahead and check them out. I have borrowed money from them, and it's super easy to get approved. They lend money to borrowers with credit scores as low as 525. You do not need good credit to access these funds.

Lastly, another great resource is the Small Business Administration, the SBA. I know so many people are intimidated by the SBA because they feel like they need to have great credit to receive approval, but don't let that deter you. They have some great programs out there for small businesses, and you want to check them out. You can get your business certified as a minority-owned business, as a woman-owned business, all right there on the SBA website. Additionally, they'll give you access to the companies that they partner with and tell you how to get even more funds if you sign up for their newsletters. SBA is a great resource for businesses. Make sure you are tapping into sba.gov to access their website.

Get your free Real Estate Training today.
Visit: www.noellesfreetraining.com

Chapter Recap

Handling Your Business Properly

- **Set up your business registration and incorporate it** with your state, choosing either a Limited Liability Company (LLC), S Corp or a C Corp.

- **File for your Employer Identification Number**, also known as your EIN. You can do this by visiting irs.gov to have your free EIN generated for you.

- **Establish a professional online presence.** Create a professional appearance by adding a professional phone number, a professional email and a website to your repertoire.

- **Seek funding for your business through grants and forgivable loans.**

- Have a written plan detailing how the money will be utilized. You will increase your chances of receiving funding if you specify the funding will be utilized for equipment purchases.

Notes:

_____

_____

Chapter 10

BUILDING BUSINESS CREDIT

> "Ninety percent of all millionaires become so through owning real estate."
>
> —Andrew Carnegie

DO YOU FEEL MORE knowledgeable about how to succeed in your real estate investor business now? I hope so. I have been laying it on pretty thick in hopes that you will become excited and more ready than ever. Before you step out and invest, there is still more helpful information I want to provide you with to ensure that you will never have any reservations about building your business credit.

I don't want your personal credit to cause you to feel stuck because it still seems like a huge barrier for you.

As your millionaire and success coach, I want to give you a few more millionaire secrets before we close out this book. I am going to share the cheat code with you to get $10,000 worth of credit in just a few months. This is more of the real strategies and systems I have personally used to help me build my business credit and open up more opportunities to grow my business using OPM.

When we talk about business credit and personal credit, there is a big difference between the two, and I need you to understand the vital concept before we head on to getting credit for you to start your business. Let's start with the personal credit. Now, you must have heard of FICO scores, right? How about Experian, Transunion, and Equifax? Yes, these are the credit bureau agencies for your personal credit. But guess what? When it comes to business credit, they have nothing to do with it.

Personal credit and business credit are two autonomous bodies. The agency that exists in the business credit realm does not exist in the personal credit realm. In business credit, the agency is named Dun and Bradstreet. This company has been around and in use for hundreds of years. Not only do the agencies differ, but the spending patterns of the credit on both sides are also completely opposite.

Let me explain what I mean. If you use a personal credit card and your limit is $1,000, and you use the entire limit, your credit score will drop, even if you make timely payments. This is how it works in the world of personal credit; they do not want you to use the max credit limit. But if you take the business credit side, they want you to use the maximum, and when you make timely payments, they see that and appreciate your business. In the world of personal credit, you will be penalized for maxing out your cards; however, in the business credit side, you will be noted by them as a business that pays its debts on time. On the personal side, they don't want you to use all the debt and they scrutinize your debt ratio all the time. Now that we have that theory on the side, you should have a smile on your face because bad personal credit does not mean you cannot get business credit. Leave your bad personal credit horrors to the side, and let me guide you on how you can get business credit.

If you recall the last chapters, we talked about the registration of the company. Once you are registered with your business, you have completed the first step toward attaining business credit. We also talked about the EIN number and the websites, phone numbers and emails you needed to look all the more professional and knowledgeable.

Once you get your EIN, you have obtained two social security numbers. One for yourself, which is the SSN with the bad credit, and this one, which is the EIN, your business's social security number. The EIN does not have a credit history. Now that you have your business's fresh credit history, it is time for you to borrow money and pay debts. Again, if not paid on time, it can die as well. You will raise your business credit by borrowings and making on-time payments.

Millionaire Secret #33: Where to Go for Business Funding

There are sources that lend money to help you with the process of building your business credit. They are known as subprime lenders. Guess who their target market is? I'll tell you. It's start-up companies of less than two years in age. Now, if you completed everything I mentioned in the last chapter, you will have no trouble taking advantage of this opportunity. Even with your personal bad credit, they will lend you money. How does this benefit them? What's the catch? Well, you have to complete transactions with them. The names of the companies are PayPal, Square, and Kabbage. These companies are lending money to businesses like yours.

To get started, you will need to set up your PayPal, Square or Kabbage account. They will ask you if you want to register as a business or as an individual, and you must choose the business option because you are going to build your business credit. If you do not have an EIN or the registration, as we mentioned earlier, your application will not be approved. Once you enter your details, the rest of the process is a piece of cake.

One of my students listened to my advice and he registered his business. He was working full-time and did not have tons of money. When he registered with PayPal, he started completing transactions through some of his partners by sending them invoices to be paid. He used this smart method to show activity on his account. And guess what? He was able to create the transactions in the business and develop an opportunity to receive funding through PayPal. There is not a cap on transactions, and you do not really need a lot of them. PayPal just wants to make sure you are using their service and are making transactions. Why? Because they charge a certain percentage of that total amount.

If you had an invoice of $500, you would actually receive somewhere around $490. The small cut goes in their pockets. Now, you don't have to go rogue at this cut and ask why they are doing that. Remember, they are giving you business credit, so it's worth it in the end. PayPal is a financially stable company with a lot of liquidity. They are using their cash to generate additional income by giving out loans to people who need them. This company owns eBay, which is owned by Elon Musk, so the cash benefit for them is a plus.

My student used their service for three months and was approved for a working capital loan. There are two types of loans that are offered. One is a working capital loan, and the other one is a loan builder. My student was approved for $10,000 in his business's name. There was no personal credit involved. Getting approved for loans is achievable, and I can certify that he did have a bad credit score, as I had checked it myself.

Another way to receive a loan is through a secured savings account. This approach worked with another student who received $1,500. The way it works is that you can get a loan backed up by your savings account. When you open your business checking account, make sure you open a business savings account. The money from your savings may be from your 401k plan, let's say, $1,000. I can go into your savings account. And guess what? They do not care about your credit score with this. Some companies offer this with savings, but some also do it with checking accounts. Credit unions do them against Cash Deposits (CD). Banks like Wells Fargo and Bank of America will do them with your savings account. I have personally done this and have two accounts with them currently. And this is not the only good news here. This method is a great way to boost your credit score as well. Yes, bad credit will get some help by your installment loan. Make your monthly payments and, once done, boom! Your credit improves, and your information is reported to the bureaus. My student has to pay just $80 per month, and that's it. At the completion, he will get his money back. A win-win!

Vendor Credit

The next method is the one I talk a lot about; it is called vendor credit. With vendor accounts you just need to make sure your payments are being reported to Duns and Bradstreet. Not all companies will report your vendor accounts, so you need to see which ones do. I know three companies that do report to Dun and Bradstreet. They also give money to startups. These companies are Uline, Quill, and Granger. My students are getting vendor credit from them and getting 30-day credit lines. Small purchases that amount to $50 will be reported to the credit bureau. So, even if they do not give you credit, you can still make cash transactions, and they will get reported. By doing this, you will start building your business credit. Once you build your credit quickly, you can then move on to get gas cards like the Chevron or Texaco, as these normally roll out easily. Later on, you can get Walmart cards, Amazon cards, and some other store cards as well.

I want you to start establishing business credit and start borrowing money in your company's name for use in your business when you do not need it. I know it seems crazy, but go ahead and get your Dun and Bradstreet number now. To get your Dun and Bradstreet number, you must have your business registered with the secretary of state, and you must have your EIN number, professional phone number, professional email, and a professional website.

I also do not recommend using your home address. I recommend using a physical address or a virtual business address that they will accept. It's absolutely free to get a Dun and Bradstreet number for a new business. To get a Dun and Bradstreet number, visit www.mydnb.com. You must fill out their application and set up your profile. After completion, the company will mail you an identification code for your business. This usually takes a few days. Once received, log back into Dun and Bradstreet and then verify your profile. It's that simple.

The best time to borrow money is when you don't need it. If you wait until you need money, that would be the hardest time to get the money. I have witnessed my students with bad credit take anywhere from 3-6 months to build their business credit, and it was much sooner if they had good credit. With good credit it will just take a few months. By doing this, you will not have any trouble whatsoever being a successful real estate investor as you will have access to business credit for your investments.

Chapter Recap

- In business credit, the agency that keeps your business credit profile is Dun and Bradstreet

- Apply for business funding with subprime lenders because their target market is start-up companies of less than two years in age.

- Set up vendor accounts as a method to help build your business credit.

- The best time to borrow money is when you don't need it.

Notes:

_____

_____

_____

_____

_____

_____

_____

_____

Chapter 11

SUCCESS PRINCIPLES FOR MILLIONAIRES

> *"Don't look for the needle in the haystack. Just buy the haystack!"*
>
> —Jack Bogle

A CAREER IN REAL ESTATE requires more than just having good information. It requires you to think quickly and adapt to the business, making the necessary adjustments to thrive in a competitive market. I remember when I came face to face with the reality of what it took to become successful in this business, when I started fixing and flipping houses. When I decided to go all-in, I made a commitment that I would do the work necessary to create the life I knew I deserved. After I decided on what my niche was, I needed to find motivated sellers. I utilized the tactics I mentioned in the previous chapters to find people who were behind on their mortgage payments. I didn't have much money for marketing, so I put out cheap ads that read, "Are you behind on your mortgage payments?" At the time this was enough to catch the attention of motivated sellers, and before long my phone started ringing off the hook. I was filling my pipeline with houses for wholesale prices, some even selling for pennies on the dollar.

I was having a blast closing deals and making a ton of money. After a while, other investors caught on and started running the same ad. The competition showed up, and it caused a strain on my business. At the time the economy was shifting, and although we would still get a ton of calls, most of our motivated sellers were upside down in their homes. Which meant they owed more than the home was worth. I didn't know what to do when I ran across that scenario.

The real crusher was the new competition. Suddenly, every Jane and John started coming out of the woodwork, bidding up whatever properties that were good deals and squeezing all the juice (equity) out of the deals. I panicked because I didn't know how to compete against other real estate investors. If I were talking to a seller and they would call another investor, I would never win the deal. I didn't know how to compete. I was still doing deals, but things just kept getting harder and harder. To make matters worse, I was working more hours than a full-time job, and I had to do even more marketing to get deals because I wasn't converting people at a high rate. I had to talk to more than 20 people just to get a deal worth $15,000.

I needed a plan that would put me back on the fast track. I knew something had to change. I diligently searched for a solution and spent the next 12 months studying every real estate strategy, reading every real estate book, and attending more seminars and conferences than I can count on two sets of hands. I was focused intently on finding and creating a system that would give me the time and the financial freedom that I envisioned of real estate investing in the first place. Even more specifically, I wanted a solution that would allow me to bypass all the noise and do eight to ten times the number of deals I was doing, while never worrying about finding motivated sellers and still make boatloads of cash. Lofty, I know. But I didn't stop until I found a solution. What I consequently came up with ended up being far better than I could have even anticipated.

Having so much competition, I did not just stick to what everyone else was doing. I made myself into a researcher, and the results of those countless hours of research produced a method that has worked for my students and me, providing us with deals and steals of the best bargains in the market. I also learned to work with other people's money and get paid huge margins without using any credit. This helped me worry less about keeping my mortgage payments in check as I flipped houses, leased them, and sold my properties as needed.

Ultimately, adapting and overcoming have been the key factors of my success in this business. When one method no longer worked, I tried another one until I was successful. This has been a success principle that I teach my students. Never give up. When the market changes, you must be willing to try new methods.

One of the biggest mistakes that new investors make when trying to learn real estate investing and getting into the real estate investing business is that they listen to outdated information, old information that is no longer relevant. You should know that the laws, legislation, market, economy, and other things closely knitted with real estate keep changing. So, you need to find updated information rather than obsolete data. If you are reading books and using resources from 2010 or 2017, you are missing out and probably doing something wrong. Things are not the same as they were. We are changing so much and there have been so many advancements in real estate. Over time, there will be new ones to fill the shoes.

I would also caution you about watching random real estate videos. I may seem a bit personally attached to this, but please stop video hopping from one person to another. I see a lot of people doing this, and it always makes my head shake with a sigh. Watching random videos will not do you any justice. Listening to random people and too many voices and directions will leave you confused. I get it, I'm a YouTuber, but at the same time, I'm just saying that if you're going to be listening to me and what I am teaching, you should probably keep me as your guidance. Because if you start to listen to everyone, you are going to take all the different formulas and recipes and make something you won't be proud of.

I am not trying to be judgmental here as there is sometimes great information out there, but you have to stay focused, as we talked about in earlier chapters. If you are listening to everyone and then using the best information you can find, trust me, the cake will not turn out like you expected. This may be the reason why you are not getting the calls you wish you could. And that is not even the worst part of this. People get into legal problems by following all the gurus out there. Make sure you do not watch random videos but rather follow someone who knows what they are doing. You want someone who has tested and proven the methods before teaching you how to do them.

Another mistake I often see, and this one is a big one, is listening to broke people. You have to stop listening to broke people! I could spend so much time here as this can really determine your success as an investor. I realize you are probably not going to like this tip as it might sound a bit harsh. But my job is to be blatant and make sure you are successful. I can add a personal example to this by sharing that Kevin Harrington is my mentor. Some people say he is a billionaire; others say he is worth five hundred million. Whatever it may be, the guy surely knows what he's doing. He knows about real estate and a lot about the business world. He knows all the factors like products, branding, and marketing that we talked about earlier, like the back of his hand.

He has personally taught me so much, and I have applied and listened to his advice. Why? Because he is more successful than I am. He is somewhere I wish to be someday. He has helped me with my marketing and branding, and he has taught me how to put myself on the hot-seat by being a YouTuber. It is mentors like him, those are more successful than I am, that I have surrounded myself with. This has worked for me because it caused me to level up in my business as an investor. I stopped doing things that were not working for me. I stopped doing the things that were steering my focus to the wrong tracks, like watching TV, gossiping, talking on the phone, surfing the internet for no reason, hanging out with childhood friends (not all of them but some of them that don't have a success mindset). Being around someone of his net worth will cause your mentality to shift. Reaching new heights of success is about leveling up and surrounding yourself with people who are successful. Because of this one change, I have created the life that I have today. I live in a nice home, and I have a business that I enjoy. I'm able to help people really enjoy and appreciate my time. I don't have to work for other people, and I can support myself and my family doing what I want to do, which is real estate investing. I can be a real estate entrepreneur and write books about it and do what I love doing.

Long story short, I had and still have mentors and friends who are more successful than I am. I don't mind being around them because they open new worlds for me. They stretch my capacity to dream bigger. This was hard for me at the beginning of my journey, as I was always the poorest person in the room. I was surrounded by people who were always talking about amounts of money that were out of my league. But guess what I did? I did not let that inferiority complex settle in. I persisted in hanging out with this superior crowd, and I talked with them. They shared their information with me and mentored me. Yes, there were times when I had to pay for their mentorship, and that is quite understandable. They were rich folks with too little time on their hands. I paid them to get a chance to learn from them. With these paid mentors, there were some who did not charge and became great friends to me. Listen, this is not rocket science. Surround yourself with successful people and listen to people that have wealth. Listen to people who have done something in their business and are making good money.

In the opening of this book, I mentioned how having the wrong mindset will limit you from building your million-dollar business. Everything starts with your mind. Everything starts with the way you think. And I'm going to be really clear: you're not going to be able to attract those successful people, people that have wealth, who have a successful business and are actually doing something, if you don't make this major adjustment. I am not talking about those fake entrepreneurs that are out here, but someone who's actually doing something. You are not going to get access to the right people unless you change the way you think. Look at yourself in the mirror and do an assessment. There are way too many fake entrepreneurs that still work a job and live paycheck to paycheck, running around telling everybody that they're an entrepreneur. But they aren't, and they have the wrong mindset. I think people take it too far when they say, "fake it until you make it." Fake it until you make it doesn't mean fake lying about your success. It's not about making it to some imaginary finish line. You actually need to be actively working on creating the business you want. Create the lifestyle you want and put in the work through inspired action to get the result that you want. It all starts with your mind.

If you think that you can't do this, then you can't be successful. If you think people that are successful have miserable lives, then that's what you'll get. But as soon as you start to change your mind and the way that you think, and you say to yourself, "I can do this, real estate investing is real, wholesaling is real, fixing and flipping is real, equity partnering is real, deals are real, and the money is there," then that is when you are ready.

The only difference between someone successful in real estate investing and someone who is unsuccessful in real estate investing is their mindset. Trust me, I've mentored hundreds of people, including men and women over the past few years. Yes, I'm new to YouTube, but I am not new to coaching. And I'm going to be really honest with you, the students who come to me who have the wrong mindset, I don't even mentor them. If you don't believe that you can have money, and that you can be wealthy, then there's nothing I can do for you. There's nothing I can teach you. You're not going to implement it. Because the difference between my successful students and my unsuccessful students is their beliefs; it is their mindset.

When a successful wholesaler gets a phone call, their mind tells them, *I'm going to convert this person.* What does an unsuccessful person do? They don't do the work.

They are afraid to make any phone calls or send their letters. They don't put out their ads on Craigslist, and they do not put out their bandit signs. Unsuccessful people are unsuccessful for a reason, and successful people are successful for a reason.

You must possess the success mentality of challenging yourself and dreaming big. If you do not have the mentality to become a successful real estate investor, you will never become one. The mind is essential to control first before you start with your wealth-building journey. Your mentality should be positive and assiduous. You also must be willing to be consistent and show up every day. You must be willing to bet on yourself, especially on those days when you don't feel successful.

Obtaining the level of wealth you want to achieve will require you to be consistent in your real estate business. Everything taught in this book is doable and highly attainable, so please make a promise to yourself that you will show up every day in your life, ready to tackle life by the horns. When I left my corporate America job making six figures, I was determined to turn my side hustle into a full-time business. I started researching all the different ways I could grow my real estate investment company. Through my mentors, I was exposed to more than wholesaling and fix and flip properties. I discovered there were multiple ways to create substantial and consistent income.

When you have made the well-calculated decisions that will help you achieve your goals, it is time to remain focused. If you have a mentality to succeed but are not keeping consistent with the milestones toward your goals, then you are not going to be successful in achieving what you aspire to. Keep a positive mentality, and then be consistent. This is a must to make sure you are maximizing your true earning potential.

Choosing the right environment is also very important. The people you associate yourself with on a daily basis will be a monumental factor in your goal of becoming a successful real estate investor.

**"Show me your friends and I will
show you your future." - Dan Pena**

As you build your new life, you have to make sure you are surrounded by people who are supportive rather than success-repellants. If you hang around pessimistic people, your financial and mental success will be challenged, resulting in a negative impact on your life. Remove yourself from anyone or any situation that prohibits you from being your best self. Make sure you are always surrounded by the right people. The right mentality, consistency in your business, and positive environment will give you the proper foundation to creating abundance.

You don't need to be a lone ranger to have success. This is a common mistake I see many newbie real estate investors making. I have a lot of hats that I wear in my business and personal life, and I still partner with other investors. Partnering with season investors will help you go further, faster. I want you to partner with someone who is experienced and knows what they're doing. Partner with someone who is going to protect you. And trust me on this one, partnering with someone who doesn't know what they're doing is never going to work. I hear people say, "We're strong and independent people." I applaud them for exhibiting the burning zeal and passion, but trying to do wholesaling all by yourself with no idea of what you're doing is a big *no!*

Chapter Recap

- Being able to adapt and overcome has been the key factor of my success in this business.

- Never listen to outdated information—old information that is no longer relevant.

- Stop watching random real estate videos. Listening to random people and too many voices and directions will leave you confused.

- Stop listening to broke people.

- Surround yourself with successful people and listen to people who have wealth and who have done something in their business. Listen to people who are making good money.

Notes:

_____

_____

_____

_____

_____

_____

Chapter 12

GET RICH WITH
REAL ESTATE

> *"It's not whether you're right or wrong that's important, but how much money you make when you're right and how much you lose when you're wrong."*
>
> —George Soros

BEFORE WE CLOSE OUT this book together, I want to leave you with a few last millionaire success principles. You have learned the ins and the outs of real estate investing. You're aware of how real estate works, the types of properties to select, and the mistakes to avoid. I want to take it a step further and teach you to think like an entrepreneur. To become rich in real estate, you have to become a real estate investor. Why do I say that? Instead of only being a real estate agent and representing people who own or want to buy properties, or being that middleman who helps facilitate the transaction for a commission, you could be the actual person who owns those properties and can receive greater profits. You could be the person who owns it and fixes it, and then later flips it. Think about it. That is pure cash coming toward you and not just a commission. You could be the landlord and receive rentals each month. Having this mentality and business savvy is how you will create your gold mine.

Have you ever asked, *How do people get rich in real estate?* I did. As a matter of fact that was the question I asked in my parents' basement after I had lost all of my properties and my money. When I got back into real estate, one of the things that I needed to learn was how other people did not lose all of their properties. How did other people continue making money when I had lost everything? There weren't a lot of people making a lot of money, but there were definitely some, and I found them. I learned they were real estate investors. I also learned that unlike me, these people had a plan. Every successful person plans, and your real estate business will require a plan as well. I know what you're thinking. This sounds super-easy, right? You're probably saying, "Of course, I plan." But I'm going to take that a step further. Don't just make a plan. Write out your plan, think about your plan, work on your plan, stick to your plan, and stay focused. This is how your dreams will begin to manifest. Take the time to appreciate your plan as it comes to life. Also, I don't want you to work so hard that you never have time to enjoy the process. I know there are people who teach you that you have to grind hard to get the things you want, but I don't believe that. I do not believe that you have to struggle and work really hard to be successful.

Millionaire Secret #34: When You Learn...Teach Others

Once I built a substantial income in real estate and quit my six-figure job, I built my rental portfolio. When my income became stable, I started teaching other people what I knew. I didn't do it on a big scale, and I didn't charge very much. I would just show new investors my properties and give them pointers. If I were doing a fix and flip, I would charge them a small cost to come view how I did it. I would show them all the paperwork, all the numbers, and I would tell them everything that I did. I even provided them with referrals to the contractors I worked with. Trust me. This was very valuable information. I did this because, as I mentioned before, you're not going to learn real estate investing by watching those TV shows. You will have to learn and then practice it yourself to master it.

I created an additional stream of income this way. When you learn all you need to know about real estate investing, build your rental properties, do your fix and flips, or wholesales, or whatever it is that you do—master it, and then teach it to others. That's going to be another stream of revenue for you. You can also write books if you don't want to teach it, as I do on YouTube. By writing books about it, you can earn money from your expertise as well. I earn money from my podcast, my YouTube page, and from my courses. I also create revenue from affiliates and others who sell my courses. What I am telling you is that I make a ton of money just teaching people what I do every day. It's just that simple, and that's how you get rich in real estate too.

Millionaire Secret #35: Use Forced Appreciation to Increase Profits

Appreciation is a smart way you can build wealth in the real estate market, much different from some other investment vehicles. One of the things you want to be careful about and take into consideration before you purchase property is the location of your properties. We have talked about appreciation and how important it is as a decisive factor for investors. You should always invest and buy properties that are increasing in value. Remember, this is not a car, a purse, or a pair of shoes. It's real estate, and you want it to appreciate.

Appreciation is so important when we're talking about getting rich. This is a method I capitalized on, and I continue to use. Buying properties at one value and doing things like forced appreciation, which is fixing the property up, adding value to it and then selling it at a higher value, is a strategy that has created considerable wealth for me.

Okay, I know I blew past that one quickly, so I'll explain it more in-depth. Let's say, I purchase a property and it's below market, but it just needs a little work. If I purchase the property for $100,000, and I put $20,000 into the property with new stainless-steel appliances, paint on the walls, and remodeled floors, then I will increase the property value. With these new additions I can sell the property for $200,000. Even with $10,000 in carrying costs, I could still walk away with $70,000 in profit. I'm giving you this example because I've done this repeatedly. Profits like this are not difficult to achieve with forced appreciation. Simply put, you "force" the property to appreciate more than it's worth by putting in equity and other things to increase the overall value.

Millionaire Secret #36: Use Leveraged Appreciation

The second type of appreciation is leveraged appreciation. This is the amazing thing about real estate and why it has created many millionaires, including me. I give credit to leveraged appreciation.

Leverage in real estate is using borrowed money to purchase a property. When leveraging a property, you borrow funds from a lender or creditor to purchase an investment property instead of having to cover the entire purchase price yourself. It is one way to increase the potential return of an investment without using your own money. The most common way to leverage your investment is through a mortgage. Usually, you would have a tenant in the property paying the mortgage, and you would receive any additional profit. This is a win-win because you don't pay much money out of your pocket, as the rental contract is covering the debt. Does this make sense? This is another way to get rich in real estate, especially if you do this over and over.

Again, I am telling you this once more: you are not going to get rich with just one rental property. I'm sorry, but that's probably the problem most people have. Leverage works best to your advantage when real estate values rise. If you have more rental properties, then you have more properties to leverage. This is the type of enterprise thinking I want you to incorporate into your real estate business. Remember the mindset we talked about at the beginning of this book? Thinking too small with one or two rental properties takes you in the opposite direction of creating millions in real estate. In fact, it's probably more of a headache than it is a business. From today I am encouraging you to think bigger—think in terms of more properties because appreciation is very real.

Millionaire Secret #37: Get Rich With Your Cash Flow

We've discussed cash flow in the previous chapters, but I really want to emphasize how important this is to help you make profit in the millions in real estate. Cash flow is money coming in that you did not work for. You are familiar with the earned income where you report to a job. This is the traditional job, even if you're a doctor or a lawyer. That's earned income. But cash flow, passive income, is from your assets. If you have a rental property that is bringing in cash flow each month that you did not have to work for, that is how you're going to get rich. You have an asset that is actually making you money. People don't realize this, but most people get rich, not by earning the money, but letting their assets earn it for them. You literally can use debt as money. Rich people turn debt into their own money. Rich people don't care about debt, which is the opposite of what most of us were taught.

I know I wasn't taught that, and that's why I just kept going to school, earning multiple degrees and trying to climb the corporate ladder to get rich. But that's not how it works. After I hired a coach and I started talking to people who were actually wealthy and had millions of dollars, I sat there wondering why I was broke every two weeks. The answer was they were not afraid of debt, and I was. They were more concerned with their cash flows. You too should do the same thing with your property. Stop focusing and worrying so much about the debt. Realize that you can turn that debt into cash flow.

Millionaire Secret #38: Focus on Residential Real Estate

One of the things that I have found from my experience and from education is that residential real estate, either single-family homes or apartments, is one of the steadiest and most lucrative types of real estate year after year. Now, commercial real estate does have its ups and downs. But when we're comparing residential to commercial real estate, residential has been the number one steadiest type of real estate investment out there. I encourage you to focus on that.

Millionaire Success Principles

On your journey to millionaire status, always remain positive and appreciative. When you work your plan and keep it at the forefront of your mind, you will begin to see it manifest. That is the process of manifestation. For lack of a better term, it's planning. I want to take this a step further and challenge you to start every day off this way. This is so important. When you wake up in the morning, you are setting the intention for your day. You want to begin with appreciation, giving gratitude for the things that you already have and the things that are coming your way. When you're positive and you're happy about what those things are, you manifest them. Because you are in a state of appreciation and you're giving gratitude for what you already have, you're being thankful for things that are yet to come—nothing specific, but just the feeling of gratitude and appreciation, and being positive—then this attitude will propel you forward. Did you know that you can change your life and that you create your own life's circumstances? This attitude is the precursor to living your life in abundance.

No matter what arises on your road to millions, always commit to your goals. You want to remain committed not just to setting goals but to executing and implementing those goals. You need to have dedication and an unwavering faith and commitment. You can't allow yourself to be easily deterred by toxic things that happen or by someone saying something negative to you. You're not going to fall for the distraction, right? Because you're committed and you know without a shadow of a doubt that whatever you believe is going to happen for you. What others have to say is none of your concern.

In addition to having a plan, staying positive, and committing to executing your goals, another success principle that millionaires practice is making decisions quickly. As a real estate investor, you will begin to see that good deals do not wait around for people to make decisions. You want to make sure that you become an expert at analyzing properties. Quickly decide whether you're in or out. You really want to get good at knowing your resources. Know which websites you're going to go to so that you can quickly evaluate whether or not you are looking at a good deal or if you're wasting time. If you are someone who takes a long time to make decisions, or you hem and haw about things, you're probably not going to be very successful as a real estate investor. Making a decision quickly is vital and should be taken into the greatest consideration.

The best time to start is now. Go ahead and pick up the phone and start building your business today. Become comfortable speaking over the phone. Practice your sales pitch and create an environment to win. So many people become flustered by speaking to sellers over the phone. Become confident and believe in yourself, so you don't have to be intimidated. Besides, the phone is where you're going to get most of your deals. You don't necessarily have to do a lot of things face to face. I believe this may be an unspoken success principle, but you have to become comfortable with speaking over the phone. Don't be afraid or shy to talk to strangers. This is the only thing separating you from your deal. You need to be willing to dial as well as answer when potential motivated sellers reach out to you. If you don't learn this success principle, then you will lose out to someone who isn't afraid. And you definitely don't want that to happen.

My Message to You

Congratulations to you for completing this book. If you put into practice the Millionaire Secrets I have revealed to you, you will become a millionaire real estate investor. I have attempted to disseminate all the vital components in as much detail and candor as I could. These lessons are things people pay hundreds and thousands of dollars to learn, and I have shared all at a mere exchange of a few bucks.

As a mother of five, I am living the golden days of my life, and I wish that for you and your family as well. I just need you to be clear-headed, to aim high and commit to the idea of success. Keep following your successful mentors, and you will reach the heights you always dreamed of. I have given you all the tools you need. Now, it is on you whether you use these tools to mine gold or to continue hitting that one stone again and again.

As we have come to the end of this journey together, I hope that you have found the information I shared throughout this book to be helpful. Your trip to real estate investor has just started, and I want you to surmount the challenges and succeed. I must be transparent and tell you that being successful in real estate is not for the faint of heart. Anything worth having will take a high level of commitment and the ability to show up for yourself and fight hard. But I am sure you already know this. Are you ready to take your first BIG STEP? You can do this! Let's go.

Chapter Recap

- Whatever it is you do, master it, and then teach it to others. That's going to be another stream of revenue for you.

- Use the forced appreciation method to increase your profits.

- Leveraged appreciation is one way to increase the potential return of an investment without using your own money.

- Residential real estate, either single-family homes or apartments, have been one of the steadiest and most lucrative types of real estate year after year.

- Success principles include *planning, staying positive, committing to executing your goals, making decisions quickly,* and *speaking comfortably* on the phone.

- The best time to start is now. Go ahead and pick up the phone and start building your business today

Notes:

_____

_____

ABOUT THE AUTHOR

NOELLE RANDALL, MPS, MBA, is an entrepreneur, real estate investor, author, speaker and all-around leader who is here to help!

Noelle is all about growth. She has been a thriving entrepreneur for over 20 years and is a successful businesswoman, renowned children's author, and real-estate entrepreneur. Her diverse business experience has been instrumental in her personal success as well as the success of countless people across the country.

She teaches real estate investing to women from varying backgrounds who are ready to transform their financial status. Noelle is a full-time real estate investor and founder of the Women Who Win in Real Estate Coaching Program. She provides training, workshops, and events to teach how to start from scratch and build a successful real estate investing business.

As CEO of Noelle Randall Coaching, Noelle offers entrepreneurs business opportunities, allowing hundreds to create wealth and financial independence through her mentorship. She has also created the opportunity to become an owner of properties across the country and obtain passive income with her company Nuurez Inc. Through her work in Nuurez, Noelle is taking the home-sharing economy to the next level! She is also the Executive Director of the Marley Simms Foundation, a public non-profit organization dedicated to promoting children's literacy. Its mission is to advance the diversity of thought in children by providing access and awareness to books from diverse authors and discussing diverse topics.

Noelle is the founder and president of FDR Horizon Enterprises, a private real estate equity firm and brand manager. The company owns a diverse portfolio of real estate and has created numerous profitable and top-selling brands, including her signature product Tea More Skinny (TeaMoreSkinny.com). Noelle is the co-founder of Bella J Hair (BellaJHair.com), the premier virgin hair extension brand and international hair and wig distributor.

In addition to being a tenacious entrepreneur and businesswoman, Noelle considers herself a perpetual student, always learning and growing. Noelle proudly boasts two advanced degrees. She earned her bachelor's degree from the University of Connecticut in Urban Planning. She has a master's degree in Economic Development from Penn State and, most recently, she earned a Master's in Business Administration (MBA) from Baylor University.

Noelle is also the proud mother of seven children, whom she credits as her inspiration for every endeavor.

CONNECT WITH NOELLE

"To reach a new level of success in what you do, you should learn all about that one thing, do it and become an expert. Once you are an expert, you can monetize something that already makes you money!"

—Noelle Randall

NOELLE RANDALL, MPS, MBA, is an engaging, transparent, and powerful speaker for audiences wishing to learn real estate and live the lives they have always wanted.

Noelle is always willing to help and teach new methods and techniques to those who might actually need it. She incorporates her teachings into her life. She does not hesitate educating people about the secrets to becoming a millionaire in real estate. Her goal is to help and make more millionaires like her.

Noelle is devoted to helping more people, and she can be sought through her website *www.noellerandall. com* or her social media accounts:

facebook.com/noellerandallcoaching

https://twitter.com/noelle_randall

https://www.instagram.com/noellerandallcoaching/

https://youtube.com/c/noellerandall1

contact@noellerandall.com

Get your free Real Estate Training today.
Visit: www.noellesfreetraining.com

ACKNOWLEDGEMENTS

I WANT TO THANK my millionaire coaches and students who have given me knowledge and insight that I am now able to share with others. I know how important you all were for me and I am grateful to be able to be that person for many others.